A to Z of Law
in
Management

A to Z of Law in Management

Maj Gen Nilendra Kumar
Judge Advocate General, Indian Army

&

Neha Chaturvedi

Manas Publications
New Delhi-110 002 (INDIA)

MANAS PUBLICATIONS
(Publishers, Distributors, Importers & Exporters)
4858, Prahlad Street,
24, Ansari Road, Darya Ganj,
New Delhi - 110 002 (INDIA)
Ph.: 23260783, 23265523 (O); 27131660,
Fax: 011-23272766
E-mail: manaspublications@vsnl.com
Web site: www.manaspublications.com

2004

ISBN 81-7049-181-9
Rs 595/-

Typeset at
Manas Publications

Printed in India at
Nice Printing Press
and Published by Mrs Suman Lata for
Manas Publications, 4858, Prahlad Street,
24, Ansari Road, Darya Ganj,
New Delhi - 110 002 (INDIA)

Dedicated

To

my wife Rekha

Foreword

Management House; 14, Institution Area
Lodhi Road, New Delhi 110003

When the authors of the Book first approached me seeking Foreword, my first reaction was to felicitate them for the venture undertaken. I further enquired why they had chosen to keep only the management professionals as their target readers. Management professional at all levels need as much to be familiarized with the basics of legal procedures and law structures. I am happy my suggestion has been readily accepted by them.

Law is essentially a rule of actions established by authority. A manager has to function within the limits of authority. There is, an imperative need for a management professional to function within its four corners. That will help him in attaining his mission in conducive environment and without legal hurdles. Law is also meant to convey a theoretical principle extracted from practice or observations. Management, on the other hand, is the process of optimum utilization of all the resources to achieve the organizational goals. A juxtaposition of the two lays bare the importance of understanding the academic essentials tested on the crucible of practicality. This explains the importance and necessity of dissemination of legal knowledge to the managers and corporate officials.

The authors have very skillfully selected the contents of the Book to propagate the essential basic of law to the management professionals in a systematic order. The topics chosen are all relevant and fulfill the contemporary wants. The Book has carefully avoided the temptation of traversing beyond its objective and has refrained from enlarging its contents to discuss unnecessary details, which may be of interest under certain situation only to a particular category of managers. The language and style adopted by the authors is simple. The practical illustrations given to explain the logic make the study relevant and absorbing.

Maj Gen Nilendra Kumar is a well known author on military law. It is heartening to see him turn his attention to a subject that had so far remained relatively neglected. I am sure his efforts ably assisted by his daughter, a young law graduate, will be of great help to all the management professionals. The publications will serve as a text book for all connected with the managerial functions. I wish it all success.

Maj Gen DM Khurana (Retd), AVSM

Director General

All India Management Association

Preface

Our interaction with the faculty and students of management schools convinced us about a need for the corporate managers to be aware of basic law provisions. A similar view was shared by a number of judges, lawyers and law teachers. Not all the management students have background in political science and law. It is necessary for them to be familiarized with essential outlines of legal procedures and judicial framework to enable them to discharge their tasks effectively. Ignorance of law is no excuse. Although it is impracticable for a layman to be aware of every branch of law, yet he must acquaint himself with the general principles of the law of the land. We hope the book will meet the requirement.

We are deeply obliged to our publishers and specially to Mr. Vivek Garg. His persistent demand for the manuscript and a critical scrutiny of its contents left us with the little option but to complete it in the form it is.

Digital technology and new communication system have made dramatic changes in the way people transact business. Increasing use of computers and automatiion is being resorted by the corportate managers. Hence the Information Technology Act 2000 has been included in part II.

Authors

Contents

Part I

1

Why Managers Need to Know About Law?

"Organized business is a thing of law; and law is always hard and unrelenting towards the weak."

Henry Ward Beecher

While taking up the study of law for the management executives, a question commonly asked is why these executives need to know about law. It is often argued that the management cadre is not going to practice law and nor do they intend joining legal profession any other way, even indirectly.

In this regard it needs to be appreciated that the future managers may be confronted with a variety of problems that would involve legal bearing. As an entrepreneur one may succeed to set up a very efficient production center. Pricing of one's product may also conform to highly competitive standards. The company accounts may be scrupulously above board. One may have hired the best of HRD executives and a very capable marketing team to sell his products. Yet there may be a sudden change in Government policy imposing new taxes or withdrawing existing fiscal incentives. There could be an income tax demand that may significantly dip into one's profits before tax. It took a number of years for a

MNC well known for its presence in tobacco and hospitality sector to fully sort out huge demands made upon it by the excise authorities. There could be legal hurdles of a variety of nature.

The management may face a notice from provident fund or labour commissioner. A company may be criticized on the ground that its advertisement offends public morality and thereby it may have to encounter a challenge for obscenity. A case in point is Kama Sutra condoms. There could be a situation where rules on intellectual property rights may create legal impediments with regard to research, development and production of certain items. There could be situations to be confronted where criminal liabilities or action is initiated against a company for torts. Incidents like the Bhopal gas tragedy involving the Union Carbide is too well known to need recapitulation. Industrial units in Agra and Delhi had to encounter major problems sometime back on account of perceived environmental threats to the Taj Mahal and Yamuna river respectively.

It is, therefore, obvious that any responsible and pro-active manager has to be aware and alive to legal provisions. He should be able to face and get across different situations so as to protect corporate interests of his organization effectively.

Well, it may be said that a company can easily hire competent lawyers to take care of its legal matters. But it is to be appreciated that in such situations one may not feel very secure if one has to totally rely upon the integrity and calibre of its solicitors and lawyers. Would the company like to be a mere spectator while its lawyer try to bail you out or combat the corporate battle on its behalf. Even with top rate lawyers of proven competence and impeccable integrity, it would always be desirable for the corporate executives to be fully integrated and involved in identifying the problem to decide the optimum strategy to find the best workable plan to achieve their object. More often than not a common sense approach in getting over complex and tricky situations would be more advantageous.

It is therefore essential that all corporate managers have a working knowledge of the legal system. They should understand the basic judicial structure and the processes involved.

What is law?

The Oxford English Dictionary defines the word "Law" as the rule made by authority for the proper regulation of a community or society or for correct conduct in life. According to Goethe, "Law alone can give us freedom." Sir William Erle said, "The law is for the protection of the weak more than the strong." In the words of Woodrow Wilson, "Law is that portion of the established habit and thought of mankind which has gained distinct and formal recognition in the shape of uniform rules backed by the authority and power of the Government." It denotes rules and principles either enforced by an authority or self-imposed by members of a society to control and regulate people's behaviour with a view to securing justice, peaceful living and social security. Nani Palkhivala has written that, "Law is a great anthropological document. It reflects man's sense of order and justice; embodies rules and traditions which hold society together; and supplies the enduring element, the dimension of performance in history." Salmond remarked, "Law is the body of principles recognized and applied by the State in the administration of justice." Great thinkers have applied their minds to different aspects concerning law. For example,

Its absence. "Without law, civilization dies" -Jewish folk saying.

Aim. "The aims at perfection" – Latin legal phrase.

Creation & Reach. "Laws are made by the conqueror and accepted by the conquered." -Latin Proverb.

Need to Enforce "Laws that are not enforced........are bad laws". Lionel J Castillo and so on.

Mercantile or Business Law —The term "mercantile law" may be defined as that branch of law which comprises laws concerning trade, industry and commercial affairs.

Management Law. The term refers to the legal provisions concerning the act of running and controlling business. Managerial law is the one connected with the work of a manager. This branch of law facilitates the act or skill of dealing with people or situations in a successful way.

2

Doctrines and Constitutional Provisions

" .... the Constitution of the United States is not a mere lawyers' document; it is a vehicle of life, and its spirit is always the spirit of the age".

Woodrow Wilson

Constitution

The Constitution is the mother of all laws. All enactments have to fall in line with it and are legally obliged to conform to its provisions. This is the basic legal doctrine of the country. The Indian Constitution, adopted by the Constituent Assembly on November 26, 1949 is a comprehensive document containing 395 Articles and nine Schedules. No Constitution in the world is perhaps so elaborate. Besides dealing with the structure of government, the Constitution makes detailed provisions for the rights of citizens and other persons in a number of entrenched provisions. It also sets forth the provisions to be followed by the State in the governance of the country, labelled as 'Directive Principles of the State Policy' and the Fundamental Duties. The Constitution is a part of the great heritage of every Indian. Its founding fathers wanted to ensure that even while India remained poor in per capital income, it should be rich in individual freedom.

The Preamble of the Constitution is the key to its social, political and economic philosophy. It enshrines sovereignty of the people, promises a socialist, secular, democratic republic based on justice, liberty, equality and fraternity. Democracy, rule of law, constitutionalism and respect for minority rights are essential, collective, inter-dependent, indivisible elements of a pluralist society. They together assure the dignity of the individual and unity and integrity of the nation. The Preamble is a part of the Constitution Statute, but it is not a part of the Constitution. The Preamble, from its very nature and content, is incapable of being amended.

The imperatives of social democracy recognize liberty, equality and fraternity as the principles of life and which cannot be divorced from each other : Liberty cannot be divorced from equality; equality cannot be divorced from liberty. Nor can liberty and equality be divorced from fraternity. Without equality, liberty would produce the supremacy of the few over the many. Equality without liberty would kill individual initiative. Without fraternity, liberty and equality could not become a natural course of things.

The Constitution deals with the election, powers, responsibilities etc of the President, Vice President, Council of Ministers and other in the executive of the Union and of the States including the Judiciary, Parliament and State Legislatures. It caters for the Union Territories, Panchayats, Municipalities, relations between the Union and the estate, finance, property, contracts and suits, trade, commerce and intercourse within the territory of India, services under the Union and the States, Tribunals, elections. Special provisions relating to certain cases, official language, emergency provisions and lastly amendment of the Constitution also exist.

All governmental organs and institutions owe their origin to the Constitution and derive their powers from its provisions. They enjoy only such powers as are conferred on them and function within limits demarcated by the Constitution. The Constitution is the supreme law of the land and its source is the people of India who have solemnly resolved to constitute India into a Sovereign Democratic Republic. It contains several distinctive features. Firstly, the Constitution of India does not envisage dual citizenship. A major change attempted recently by the executive is the plan to permit Non-Resident Indians or those of Indian origin to avail the status of Indian citizenship. Secondly, the Constitution provides for single constituent authority. The States do not have the right to make their own Constitution. Thirdly, it minimizes rigidity and legalism. Fourthly, in normal times the Constitution is framed to work as a federal system but in times of war and other national emergencies, it is designed to work as though it were unitary. Fifthly, it maintains unity in basic matters. The High Court and the Supreme Court form a single integrate judiciary having jurisdiction over all cases arising under various laws – Union, State, constitutional, civil and criminal. There is uniformity in fundamental laws, civil and criminal. To maintain uniformity in administration, the Constitution provides that there shall be All India Services including Judicial Services, recruited on an all India basis which shall be common to the Union and the States. Sixthly, our Constitution does not set up the States as rivals to one another or to the Union. One of the essential features of the Constitution is that no State legislature can amend the fundamental rights or any other part of the Constitution. The limited amending power of Parliament which was limited to preserve and protect the basic feature of the Constitution is itself a fundamental feature of the Constitution.

Definition of State

In the context of fundamental right, "State" includes–

1. The Government and Parliament of India.
2. The Government and the legislature of each of the States; and
3. All local or other authorities within the territory of India or under control of the Government of India to include–
   (a) Municipal Boards.
   (b) Panchayats.
   (c) Improvements Trusts; and
   (d) Port Trusts.
   (e) All authorities created by the Constitution or some statute and on whom powers are Committee or Corporations.
   (f) District conferred by law e.g. a university.

Fundamental Rights

"The laws assist those who are vigilant, not those who sleep over their rights".

Legal Maxim

The rights available to the people under the Constitution can be divided into two types viz Fundamental Rights and Constitutional Rights. On the other hand, those flowing from other enactments are called Statutory Rights. The Constitution embodies a list of fundamental rights. These rights are not in absolute terms but are subject to the limitations which are expressly defined by the Constitution itself. Some of the fundamental rights can only be claimed by a citizen of India whereas others apply equally to non-citizens also. A fundamental right as defined in the Constitution differs from a non-fundamental right in one vital respect, a fundamental right (subject to the qualifications defined in the Constitution itself) is inviolable, whereas a non-fundamental right possesses no such characteristics. It is inviolable in the sense that no law, ordinance, custom, usage or administrative order can abridge or take away a fundamental right. A law which violates any of the fundamental right is void. A fundamental right cannot be taken away even by a constitutional amendment if it forms the basic structure of the Constitution. Some of the fundamental rights which are relevant for the purpose of this topic are enumerated below.

Article 14. Right to Equality. The State shall not deny to any person equality before the law or equal protection of the laws within the territory of India. This article makes the concept of equal treatment a binding principle of State action. All persons and things similarly circumstanced shall be treated alike both in privileges and liabilities imposed. It means that amongst equals the law should be equal and should be equally administered and that like should be treated alike.

Prohibition of discrimination on grounds of religion, race, caste, sex or place of birth. The relevant clauses are (1) to (3) which lay down:

(1) The State shall not discriminate against any citizen on grounds only of religion, race, caste, sex, place of birth or any of them.

(2) No citizen shall, on ground only of religion, race, caste, sex, place of birth or any of them be subject to any disability, liability, restriction or condition with regard to:-

(a) access to shops, public restaurants, hotels and places of public entertainment; or

(b) the use of wells, tanks, bathing ghats, roads and places of public resort maintained wholly or partly out of State funds or dedicated to the use of the general public.

(3) Nothing in this Article shall prevent the State from making any special provision for women and children. The right guaranteed in clause (1) is conferred on a citizen as an individual and is available against his being subjected to discrimination in the matter of rights, privileges and immunities pertaining to him as a citizen generally.

In view of the clause (2), there cannot be shops or public restaurants or other places of public entertainment like cinema, theatre, coffee house, circus, fair, exhibition, music hall, race course etc exclusively reserved for members of a particular caste, religion or race.

Article 16. Equality of opportunity in matters of public employment

(1) There shall be equality of opportunity for all citizens in matters relating to employment or appointment to any office under the State.

(2) No citizen shall, on grounds only of religion, race, caste, sex, descent, place of birth, residence or any of them, be ineligible for, or discriminated against in respect of any employment of office under the State. Clause (1) applies only in respect of employments or offices which are held under the State i.e. in respect of persons holding

office as subordinate to the State. What is guaranteed is the equality of opportunity. Principle of equal pay to equal work is also covered by equality of opportunity to Article 16(1). As regards clause (2), it is to be noted that there is no constitutional prohibition against private persons or bodies preferring men of one religion to the other in making appointments.

Article 19. Protection of certain rights regarding freedom of speech etc –all citizens shall have the right:-

(a) to freedom of speech and expression;

(b) to assemble peaceably and without arms;

(c) to form Associations or Unions;

(d) to move freely throughout the territory of India;

(e) to reside and settle in any part of the territory of India;

(f) to practice any profession, or to carry on any occupation, trade or business.

Commerical speech, It has been held that commercial speech is a part of the freedom of speech and expession guaranteed under Article 19 (1) (a). Therefore, a commercial speech can also be subjected to reasonable restrictions only under Article 19 (2)and not otherwise. On that basis Tata Press Yellow Pages comprising paid advertisements from businessmen, traders and professionals was upheld as an exercise of freedom of speech and expression under Article 19 (1) (a). (Tata Press Ltd v Manager Telephone Nigam Ltd; AIR 1995 SC 2438).

Article 20. Protection in respect of conviction of offences

(1) No person shall be convicted of any offence except for violation of a law in force at the time of commission of the act charged as an offence, nor be subjected to a penalty greater than that which might have been inflicted under the law in force at the time of the commission of the offence.

(2) No person shall be prosecuted and punished for the same offence more than once.

(3) No person accused of any offence shall be compelled to be a witness against himself.

Article 21. Protection of life and personal liberty -No person shall be deprived of his life or personal liberty except according to procedure established by law.

Article 22. Protection against arrest and detention in certain cases

(1) No person who is arrested shall be detained in custody without being informed, as soon as may be, of the grounds for such arrest nor shall he be denied the right to consult, and to be defended by, a legal practitioner of his choice.

(2) Every person who is arrested and detained in custody shall be produced before the nearest Magistrate within a period of twenty four hours of such arrest excluding the time necessary for the journey from the place of arrest to the court of the Magistrate and no such personal shall be detained in custody beyond the said period without the authority of a Magistrate.

Article 32. Right to Constitutional Remedies

(1) This Article appears in the form of a guarantee. It provides a right to move the Supreme Court by appropriate proceedings for the enforcement of various rights enumerated under this Part of the Constitution.

(2) The Supreme Court shall have power to issue directions or order or writs including writs in the nature of habeas corpus, mandamus, prohibition, quo warrant and certiorari, whichever may be appropriate, for the enforcement of any of the rights conferred by this Part.

(3) Without prejudice to the powers conferred on the Supreme Court by clauses (1) and (2), Parliament may by law empower any other court to exercise within the local limits of its jurisdiction all or any of the powers exercisable by the Supreme Court under clause (2).

(4) The right guaranteed by this Article shall not be suspended except as otherwise provided for by this Constitution.

Fundamental Duties

"People tend to forget their duties but remember their rights".

Indira Gandhi

Part IVA of the Constitution of India was added by the Constitution (42nd Amendment) Act, 1976. The fundamental duties are addressed to the citizen, without any legal sanction for their violation. The citizen, it is expected, should be his own monitor while exercising and enforcing his fundamental rights, not remembering that he owes the duties enumerated in Article 51A to the State. He has to appreciate that if he does not care for the duties he should not deserve the rights.

Article 51A lays down that, "it shall be the duty of every citizen of India–

(a) to abide by the Constitution and respect its ideal and institutions, the National Flag and the National Anthem;

(b) to cherish and follow the noble ideals which inspired our national struggle for freedom; One of the noble ideals of the great visionaries and fighters for national freedom was to ensure for the country certain fundamental rights which would be inalienable and to guarantee liberties for all citizens.

(c) to uphold and protect the sovereignty, unity and integrity of India;

(d) to defend the country and render national service when called upon to do so;

(e) to promote harmony and the spirit of common brotherhood amongst all the people of India transcending religions; to renounce practices derogatory to the dignity of women;

(f) to value and preserve the rich heritage of our composite culture;

(g) to protect and improve the natural environment including forests, lakes, rivers and wild life and to have compassion for living creatures;

(h) to develop the scientific temper, humanism and the spirit of inquiry and reform; The scientific temper postulates the habit of thinking with clarity and using words with precision, and a calm and dispassionate consideration of every issue in conditions of normalcy.

(j) to safeguard public property and to abjure violence.

(k) to strive towards excellence in all spheres of individual and collective activity so that the nation constantly rises to higher level of endeavour and achievement."

The fundamental duties as such are not legally enforceable in the Courts; but if the State makes a law to prohibit any act or conduct in violation of any of the duties, the Courts would uphold that as a reasonable restriction on the relevant fundamental right.

Another interesting aspect is that the duties are not addressed to the State. Hence, a citizen cannot claim that he must be properly equipped by the State so that he may perform his duties under Article 51A. These would also serve as a warning to reckless citizens against anti-social activities such as burning the Constitution, destroying public property and the like.

Directive Principles of State Policy

The Articles included in Part IV of the Constitution (Articles 36 to 51) contain certain directives which it shall be the duty of the States to follow both in the matter of administration as well as in the making of laws. They embody the aims and objects of the State under the Republican Constitution. Most of these aim at the establishment of the economic and social democracy which is pledged for in the Constitution.

The directives, differ from the fundamental rights contained in Part III of the Constitution or the ordinary laws of the land, in that the directives are not enforceable in the courts and do not create any justifiable rights in favour of individuals. They require to be implemented by legislation. Yet, these principles have been declared to be "fundamental in the governance of the country and it shall be the duty of the State to apply these principles in making laws". It should be the duty of the Union to see that every State takes steps for implementing the Directives, as far as possible. The directive principles are so comprehensive that they operate at all levels and they cover all the significant fields of international policy, as well as of domestic policy, including social, economic, education, legal and judicial.

Examples

1. State to secure a social order for the promotion of the welfare of the 3people.
2. Certain principles of policy to be followed by the State.
3. Equal justice and free legal aid.
4. Organisation of Village Panchayats.
5. Right to work, to education and to public assistance.
6. Provision for just and humane conditions of work and maternity relief.
7. Living wage etc for workers.
8. Participation of workers in management of industries.
9. Uniform Civil Code for the citizens.
10. Provision for free and compulsory education for children.

The courts are not competent to compel the Government to carry out any directive. In case of any conflict between the fundamental rights and the directive principles, the former should prevail in the courts. Yet, these principles have been declared to be 'fundamental in the governance of the country and it shall be the duty of the State to apply these principles in making laws'. These were intended as moral precepts for the authorities of the State.

Freedom of Trade, Commerce and Intercourse

Article 19 (1) (g) guarantees that all citizens have the right to practice any profession or to carry on any occupation or trade or business. The right to carry on a business would include the right to close down or relinquish or sell the business. The right must be exercised consistently with human dignity.

Article 301 provides: "subject to other provisions of this part, trade, commerce and intercourse through the territory of India shall be free." The freedom may be defined as a right to free movement of persons or things, tangible or intangible, commercial or non-commercial, unobstructed by barriers, inter-state or intra-state or any other impediment operating as such barriers.

Trade. Trade in its widest import covers not merely "buying and selling of goods" but trading facilities like advances, overdrafts, mercantile documents and insurance and many other sophisticated operations connected with and essential for commerce and intercourse. Even travel facilities in certain circumstances have a nexus with trade and commerce.

The word business is ordinarily synonymous with the word trade. It connotes some real, substantial, systematic or organized course of activity or conduct with the purpose of earning profit.

Distinction between Constitutional Law and Statutory Law – Constitution is permanent. It is an organic statute and it grows by its own inherent force. It is a ground harm from which the statutes are derived. Statutory law is the written expression of the legislative will. It is the positive declaration of what the law shall be by that branch of the Government possessing legislative functions. The relationship between the two is of higher-lower norms. The validity of the Constitution cannot be challenged whereas the legality of an ordinary law or statutory law can be challenged on the touchstone of the Constitution.

Act-Act is a Statute or law enacted by the legislative body. General or Public Acts are those which bind the whole community e.g. The Indian Evidence Act. On the other hand, private or special Acts are those which operate upon particular persons and private persons e.g. The Army Act. A Bill is a draft or form of an Act presented to the legislature, but not enacted.

Rules-Rules are made under a certain Act and must be treated as a part of the said Act. They have the force of law and ought to be judicially noticed for purpose of construction or obligation. The purpose of the Rule is to provide for procedural matters or for such matters as are subsidiary to the provisions of the Act. In some cases they may explain the provisions of the Act, and in some cases, it may be legitimate to read the Rules along with provisions of the Act in order to find out the true intention of the legislature in enacting the latter. However, no Rule can ever be constructed to override the specific provisions of the Act itself.

Regulations–Regulations may be statutory or non statutory (administrative regulations). Statutory regulations have the force of law. They are published in the official gazette and on such publication they have the effect of enacted laws. On the other hand, non statutory (administrative) regulations are in nature of administrative instructions. All the regulations such as Regulations for the Army, Pay and Allowances Regulations, the Pension Regulations and Travel Regulations fall in the second category.

Instructions –Instructions are issued on matter concerning organization, discipline, administration and financial matter by the Central Government or a State. These are also in nature of administrative instructions and are enforceable on the authority of Government of India or the State concerned.

Order –The words 'Rule' and 'Order', when used in a statute, have a definite significance. They are different in their nature and extent. A Rule, to be valid, must be general in scope and indiscriminating in its application. The function of an order relates more particularly to the execution or enforcement of a Rule previously made. An order of a Municipality is not a law but merely the form in which the body expresses an opinion. An order is of special temporary character.

Note

3

Rules of Natural Justice

"What is hateful to you, do not to your fellow; that is the whole law; all the rest is interpretation."

Hillel, Talmund Shabbat

There may be situations where a manager is required to take decisions or undertake enquiries, where natural justice rules are needed to be observed. This could be necessitated when the conduct of a subordinate is under probe. The relationship with a dealer or supplier may call upon such a decision-making. The term 'natural justice' means that a result or process should be just. The substantial elements of natural justice must be found to have been present at the inquiry. There must be due inquiry. The accused person or the one affected by it must have notice of what for he is accused. He must have an opportunity of being heard and the decision must be honestly arrived at after he has had a full opportunity of being heard. The law recognizes three principles of natural justice :-

(a) Audi alter am partem

(b) Bias of interest, and

(c) The requirement of reasoned decision.

The rules of natural justice are not rigid norms of unchanging contents.

> **Audi alter am partem (Hear the other side).** This means that the parties be given adequate notice and opportunity to be heard.

The principle is that both the sides should have a full and fair hearing. No man should be condemned unheard. In other words, the party whose civil rights are affected in a judicial or quasi-judicial proceedings must have reasonable notice of the case he has to meet and an opportunity of stating his case. Thus, where the collector of customs passed an order of confiscation without notice and without enquiry, the order was held to be in contravention of the principles of natural justice[1]. When on the question of facts there was no dispute, no real prejudice has been caused to a party aggrieved by an order, by absence of any formal opportunities of cross examination per se does not invalidate or vitiate the decision arrived at fairly. This is more so when the party against whom an order has been passed does not dispute the facts and does not demand to test the veracity of the version of the credibility of the statement.

The object of the principles of natural justice, which are now understood as synonymous with the provision to provide a fair hearing is to ensure that justice is done, that there is no failure of justice and that every person whose rights are going to be effected by the proposed action gets a fair hearing.

A corollary to this rule implies that evidence must not be given behind the back of the other party but in his presence, so that if written evidence is given it must be made available to the other party with opportunity to contradict it. In Dhakeshwari Cotton Mills V CIT; AIR 1955 SC 65 the Supreme Court held that it was a violation of the principles of natural justice when the Income Tax Appellate Tribunal did not convey to the assessee the information which had been supplied to it by the departmental representative and to give him an opportunity to contradict it.

Bias and interest. The principles governing the doctrine of bias are that–

(i) No man shall be a judge in his own cause.

(ii) Justice should not only be done but manifestly and undoubtedly seen to be done. The interest or bias which disqualifies must be one in the matter to be litigated. A mere general interest in the general object to be pursued will not disqualify a judge. Interest is to be distinguished from favour; and favour is not to be presumed in a judge. Certain examples of favour or non-pecuniary bias which may disqualify are given below:-

- Family relationship.
- Membership of interested bodies and associations.
- Judges having acted as counsel in earlier stages of a case.
- Judges sitting in appeal from their own decisions.

If a member of a judicial body in 'subject to a bias' (whether financial or otherwise) in favour or against any party to a dispute, or is in such a position that bias must be assumed to exist, he ought not to take part in the decision or sit on the tribunal. In Khelawati V Chet Ram[2], where the tribunal consisted, among others, of very close relations and friends of one of the parties, the court set aside the proceedings under this doctrine as being contrary to the principles of natural justice.

(iii) **The requirement of reasoned decision**. The duty to give reasons may be either a statutory requirement or non-statutory. The Supreme Court in Bhagar Raj V Union of India[3] observed : "A tribunal which exercises judicial or quasi-judicial powers can certainly indicate its mind as to why it acts in a particular way, and when important rights of parties of far reaching consequence to them are adjudicated upon in a summary fashion, without giving a personal hearing where proposals and counter proposals are made and examined, the least that can be expected is that the tribunal should tell the party why the decision is going against him in all cases where the law gives a further right of appeal".

This requirement of natural justice is applicable not only to judicial or quasi-judicial orders but also to administrative orders affecting prejudicially the party in question, unless it is expressly excluded by a law which is otherwise valid. In the spheres of public employment, this means that any action taken by the employer against an employee must be fair, just and reasonable which are components of "fair treatment". Thus, the conferment of absolute power to dismiss a permanent employee is anti-thesis to just or fair treatment.

Rule of Law

Rule of law excludes arbitrariness; its postulate is 'intelligence without passion' and 'reason freed from desire.' Wherever arbitrariness or unreasonableness is found, there is a denial of rule of law. The term 'rule of law' in brief, connotes the undisputed supremacy of law, and envisages a state of things in which everyone respects the law and where law has to be followed by every one collectively and individually by the citizens as well as by the State.

Rule of law includes review of arbitrary executive action. It means, in the first place, the absolute supremacy or predominance of regular law as opposed to the influence of arbitrary power, and excludes the existence of arbitrariness, of prerogative, or even of wide discretionary.

The absence of arbitrary power is the first essential of the rule of law upon which the whole constitutional system is based. In a system governed by the rule of law, discretion, when conferred upon executive authorities, must be confined within clearly defined limits. The rule of law, from this point of view, means that decisions should be made by the application of known principles and rules, and, in general, such decisions should be predictable and the citizen should know where he is. If a decision is taken without any principle or without any rule, it is unpredictable and such a decisions is the anti-thesis of a decision taken in accordance with the rule of law.

Endnotes

1. Collector of Customs V AHA Rahiman, AIR 1957 Mad 496.
2. AIR 1952 Punj 67
3. AIR 1967 SC 1606 to 13

Note

4

Frame Work of Judicial System

"Laws are a dead letter without courts to expound and define their true meaning and operation".

Alexander Hamilton

Higher Judiciary

Judiciary is a term applied to a co-ordinated department of the Government, which construes and applies the laws; relating to that department of the Government that has to do with the expounding and administering of the law; the officers of that department that expounds and administers the law, the judges taken collectively. The laws of a free Government are construed and applied by the judiciary or judicial department. This department has distinct and independent powers, designed to operate as a check upon those of the legislative and executive departments. It is confined to its own functions, and can neither encroach upon nor be made subordinate to those of another. According to Article 50 of the Constitution, "The State shall take steps to separate the judiciary from the executive in the public services of the State". Apart from the Parliament and the executive, the judiciary is one of the three important pillars of our country. The Supreme Court is at once a Federal Court, a Court of Appeal and a guardian of our Constitution. The law declared by it, in the exercise of any of its jurisdictions under the Constitution, is binding on all other Courts within the territory of India. Higher judiciary refers to the Supreme Court of India and High Courts of various States. The Supreme Court provisions have been included in Chapter IV of the Constitution of India under the heading "The Union Judiciary." High Courts have been invested with inherent powers under the Criminal Procedure Code to make such orders as may be necessary to give effect to any order or to prevent abuse of the process of any court or otherwise to secure the ends of justice.

Subordinate Judiciary

For the purposes of the Code of Civil Procedure, the District Court is subordinate to the High Court, and every civil court of a grade inferior to that of a District Court and every court of small causes is subordinate to the High Court and District Court. A 'Revenue court' means a court having jurisdiction under any local law to entertain suits or other proceedings relating to the rent, revenue or profits of land used for agricultural purposes but does not include a civil court.

Quasi-Judicial Tribunals

The word 'quasi' when referred to a legal term generally means that the thing, which is described by the word, has some of the legal attributes denoted and connoted by the legal term, but that it has not all of them. It indicates sharing the qualities of and approximating to what is judicial, essentially judicial in character but not within the judicial power or function not belonging to the judiciary as constitutionally defined. For instance, if a transaction is described as a quasi-contract it means that the transaction, has some of the attributes of a contract but not all. Perhaps the best meaning of the word "quasi" is "not exactly". A quasi-judicial decision is thus one which has some of the attributes of a judicial decision, but not all.

A quasi-judicial decision pre-supposes an existing dispute between two or more parties and involves following requisites:-

(1) The presentation (not necessarily orally) of their case by the parties to the dispute.

(2) If the dispute between them is a question of fact, the ascertainment of the fact by means of evidence adduced by the parties to the dispute and often with the assistance of arguments by or on behalf of the parties on the evidence.

(3) If the dispute between them is a question of law, the submission of legal argument by the parties.

(4) A decision in the form of administrative action.

Tribunals

Tribunal indicates the seat of a judge or a court of justice. The term "tribunal" refers to quasi-judicial tribunals, other than the ordinary courts which have the trappings of a court. The power of adjudication has been conferred on the authority in question by statute. It discharges purely administrative or executive functions.

Article 323A of the Constitution provides for setting up of the tribunals. Examples of certain existing Tribunals are given below:-

(a) Central Administrative Tribunal.

(b) Motor Accident Claims Tribunal.

(c) Income Tax Appellate Tribunal.

(d) Industrial Tribunal.

(e) Railway Rates Tribunal.

(f) Appellate Tribunal for Foreign Exchange.

(g) Appellate Tribunal for Forfeited Property.

(h) Customs Excise & God (Control) Appellate Tribunal.

Authority

It is a body having a jurisdiction in certain matters of a public nature. Examples of certain authorities constituted by the Government are as under:-

(a) Appellate Authority for Industrial and Financial Re-construction.

(b) Authority for Advance Rulings (Tax).

(c) Competent Authority SAFEMFOPA & NDPSA.

(d) Insurance Regulatory & Development Authority.

(e) National Environment Appellate Authority.

(f) National Highways Authority of India.

(g) Telecom Authority of India.

Board

A number of persons appointed or elected to sit in council for the management or investigation of a public or private business, trust or other organization or institution is called a board. Examples:-

(a) Board for Industrial & Financial Re-construction.

(b) Central Board of Direct Taxes.

(c) Central Board of Excise & Customs.

(d) Central Pollution Control Board.

(e) Company Law Board.

(f) Copyright Board.

The selfish spirit of commerce knows no country, and feels no passion of principles but that of gain.

Thomas Jefferson

Consumer Protection Act

The Consumer Protection Act, 1986 is a milestone in the history of social economic legislation and is directed towards public welfare and public benefits. The cut-throat competition between the manufacturers and traders was found to have led to the exploitation of the consumers. The main object of the Act is to protect the genuine interest and rights of the consumers.

The Act is fast emerging as the true saviour of the rights of the consumers. The preamble to the Act provides that the Act is intended for the protection of the interests of the consumers and for that purpose to make provisions for the establishment of consumer councils and other authorities for the settlement of consumer disputes and for matters connected there with.

Consumer is one who consumes. As per the definition under Section 2(1)(d)(i), consumer is the one who purchases goods for private use or consumption. The meaning of the word 'consumer' is broadly stated in the above said definition so as to include anyone who consumes goods or services at the end of the chain of production. The comprehensive definition aims at covering every man who pays money as the price or cost of goods and services. In order to satisfy the requirement of the definition, there must be a transaction of buying goods for consideration. The definition contemplates the pre-existence of a completed transaction of a sale and purchase of goods.

The Act consists of 31 Sections. To initiate an action under the Consumer Protection Act what is required is a complaint from the complainant. A complaint can be made by a consumer; or any voluntary consumer association registered under the Companies Act, 1956 or under any other law for the time being in force; or the Central Government or any State Government, who or which makes a complaint; one or more consumers, where there are consumers having the same interest. A consumer includes any one or who consumes goods or services.

A complaint means any allegation in writing made by a complainant in regard to one or more of the following :

(i) An unfair trade practice or a restricted trade practice has been adopted by any trader;

(ii) The goods bought by him or agreed to be bought by him, suffer from one or more defects;

(iii) The Services hired or availed of or agreed to be hired or availed of by him suffer from deficiency in any respect;

(iv) A trader has charged for the goods mentioned in the complaint a price in excess of the price fixed by or under any law for the time being in force or displayed on the goods or any package containing such goods.

(v) Goods which will be hazardous to life and safety, when used, are being offered for sale to the public in contravention of the provisions of any law for the time being in force.

Consumer Disputes Redressal Agencies include the District Forum, State Commission and the National Commission. The Act, thus, envisages a three tier quasi-judicial machinery at the district, state and national level. There are monetary limits as under to invoke their jurisdiction:-

(a) **District Forum** – where the compensation does not exceed Rupees twenty slakhs. The total number of district forums is 570.

(b) **State Commission** – where the claim exceeds Rupees twenty lakhs but does not exceed Rupees one crore. There are 35 State Commissions.

(c) **National Commission** – For complaints exceeding Rupees Twenty lakhs.

The State Commission may entertain appeals against the orders of any District Forum within the State. Similarly, any person aggrieved by an order made by the State Commission may prefer an appeal against such order to the National Commission within a period of 30 days from the date of the order in such form and manner as may be prescribed. Section 23 of the Consumer Protection Act provides that any person aggrieved by an order made by the National Commission, may prefer an appeal against such order to the Supreme Court within a period of 30 days from the date of the order. The Act has not mentioned any specific grounds for making appeal to the Supreme Court. Every order of the District Forum, State Commission or the National Commission shall, if no appeal has been preferred against such order under the provisions of the Consumer Protection Act, be final.

Highlights of the important amendments brought into force from 15 March 2003. The provisions of the Act are mainly aimed at facilitating quicker disposal of complaints, enhancing the capability of redressal agencies, strengthening them with more power, streamlining the procedures and widening the scope of the Consumer Protection Act to make it more effective and purposeful. It consists of provision for issue of interim orders by redressal agencies, prescribing time-frame for admission, issue of notices and disposal of complaints/appeals, provision for service of notices by courier, fax, speed post etc, provision for senior-most Member to preside the Consumer Forum in the absence of President for any reason, provision for creation of benches in the National Commission and State Commissions for holding of circuit benches. It looks into matters relating to services utilized for commercial purposes excluded from the purview of consumer forums (goods already excluded), inclusion of sale of spurious goods/services as unfair trade practice, recover of compensation amount ordered by the redressal agency through certificate case in the same manner as arrears of land revenue and establishment of Consumer Protection Council at District level.

Detailed text of the Consumer Protection (Amendment) Act, 2002 is available at website: www.fcamin.nic.in

Lok Adalats

Legal Services Authorities Act, 1987 (Act No 39 of 1987) is the enactment in this regard.

The said Act came into force with effect from 9 Nov 1995. It has been designed to constitute legal services authorities to provide free and competent legal services to the weaker sections of the society to ensure that opportunities for securing justice are not denied to any citizen by reason of economic or other disabilities, and to organize Lok Adalats to secure that the operation of the legal system promotes justice on a basis of equal opportunity. It is noteworthy that Article 39A of the Constitution which deals with equal justice and free legal aid reads as follows. "The State shall secure that the operation of the legal system promotes Justice, on the basis of equal opportunity, and shall, in particular, provide free legal aid, by suitable legislation or schemes or in any other way, to ensure that opportunities for securing justice are not denied to any citizen by reason of economic or other disabilities".

A "Lok Adalat" means a Lok Adalat organized under Chapter VI of the aforesaid Act. The significant features are as under:-

1. It may be organized by the State or district authorities; or the Supreme Court Legal Services Committee or every High Court Legal Services Committee or Taluk Legal Services Committee.
2. To consist of judicial officers of the area and other members with prescribed qualifications and experience.

3. It enjoys jurisdiction with regard to civil, criminal or revenue matters.

4. Its award is deemed to be decree of civil court order or any other court.

5. Its order is final and binding on all the parties to the dispute. No appeal shall lie to any court.

6. It shall have jurisdiction to determine and to arrive at a compromise or settlement between the parties to a dispute, provided that the Lok Adalat shall have no jurisdiction in respect of any case or matter relating to an offence not compoundable under any law.

7. Every Lok Adalat shall, while determining any reference before it under the applicable Act, act with utmost expedition to arrive at a compromise or settlement between the parties and shall be guided by the principles of justice, equity, fair play and other legal principles.

8. (i) Every award of the Lok Adalat shall be deemed to be a decree of a Civil Court, or as the case may be an order of any other court and where a compromise or settlement has been arrived at, by a Lok Adalat in a case referred to it under Sub-Section 1 of Section 20, the Court fee paid in such case shall be refunded in the manner provided under the Court Fee Act, 1870.

   (ii) Every decisions made by a Lok Adalat shall be final and binding on all the parties to the dispute and no appeal shall lie to any Court against the award.

9. The Lok Adalat shall have same powers as are vested in a civil court under the Code of Civil Procedure in respect of summoning and enforcing attendance of a

witness and examining him on oath, the discovery and production of any documents, the reception of evidence on affidavits, the requisitioning of any public record or document.

Relevance to the Field of Management

The normal legal process entails considerable delay. The backlog of pending cases impedes speedy disposal of disputes. The process involved is expansive. Quite often it would be advantageous to avoid recourse to judicial process. There is adequate case law to demonstrate the efficacy of the Lok Adalats as a tool to settle disputes concerning management or corporate world. A few illustrative cases are given below.

(a) Insurance Sector. In New India Assurance Co Ltd V Boda Hari Singh; 1998(6) ALT 34 it was held that the Act came into force in Andhra Pradesh in October 1995 and it is prospective in operation and for taking cognizance of a case by Lok Adalat there must be a reference by the Court.

(b) Port Trust. In Board of Trustees of the Port of Visakhapatnam; 2000(5) ALD 682, it was held that the award of Lok Adalat is deemed to be decree of a civil court passed on compromise and would be final to which no appeal lies.

(c) Tourism Industry. Tourism development at the cost of environment and ecology had been deprecated; 1995 AIHC 5762 (HC).

(d) Use of Public Land. Every citizen has a fundamental right to redress the perceived legal injury through judicial process. The encroachers are no exception to that constitutional right to judicial redressal; Old Tellis case, AIR 1986 SC 180 (Para 57)

(e) Health Care & Hospitality Sector. Every person who has to file or defend a case shall be entitled to legal services under this Act, if that person is in custody in a protective home under Clause 2(g) of the Immoral Traffic (Prevention) Act or in a juvenile home or in a psychiatric hospital or psychiatric nursing home; vide Section 12(g) of Legal Services Authority Act, 1987.

(f) Catering Service. It is open to the passengers in a train not to eat food. Their not eating food will not make rail fare inclusive of catering charges unjust because the option is nonetheless open to eat food and avail of other facilities. Aptkshaben V Union of India; 1996(2) CCC 484.

(g) Steel Industry. In JK Steels Ltd V Union of India; AIR 1970 SC 1173, it was held that an affidavit containing expression of opinion in the context of general policy by Union Government cannot deemed to be an admission on a particular point.

(h) Jute Industry. In the case of New Central Jute Mills V Deputy Secretary Ministry of Finance, 1965(2) Com LJ 152, the Court declared that vague and uninformative affidavits have no value.

Company Law Board

Under Sections 10 E(1) and 637(1)(a) of the Companies Act, 1956, the Central Government has the power to constitute a Company Law Board and to delegate its functions to the Board. The Board can consist of such number of persons not exceeding five as the Government thinks fit. One of the members of the Board has to be appointed a Chairman and this necessarily implies that the Board shall consist of at least two members. To this Board the Government may delegate its function under Section 237. Section 637 shows that the function under Section 237 can be delegated to the Board and to no other authority. The function under Section 237(b) involves the exercise of a discretion. Under Sections 10 (5) and 642(1), the Central Government may frame rules regulating the procedure of the Board and generally to carry out the purposes of the Act.

Under Section 111 of the Companies Act, the Company Law Board is empowered to make orders directing rectification of the company's register as to damages, costs and incidental and consequential orders. It may decide any question relating to the title of any person who is a party before it to have his name entered upon the company's register and any question which it is necessary or expedient to decide, it may make interim orders. Failure to comply with any order visits the company with a fine. In regard to all these matters it has exclusive jurisdiction (except under the provisions of the Special Court Act). Its orders are appealable. The Company Law Board, further, is a permanent body constituted under a statute. It performs functions which are administrative, as under Sections 224 and 269, and curial, as under Section 111. In exercising its function under Section 111, it must act judicially.

Note

5

Business & Management Laws

"No cause of action arises from a bare promise."

Legal Maxim

The Indian Contract Act, 1872

Definition of Contract

According to Section 2(h) of the Indian Contract Act: "An agreement enforceable by law is a contract." A contract, therefore, is an agreement the object of which is to create a legal obligation i.e., a duty enforceable by law. A contract essentially consists of two elements:

(a) An agreement

(b) Legal obligation –a duty enforceable by law

Agreement. As per Section 2(0e), "Every promise and every set of promises, forming the consideration for each other, is an agreement." Thus 'promise' is an agreement. What is a 'promise'? The answer to this question is contained in Section 2(b) which defines the term, "When the person to whom the proposal is made signifies his assent thereto, the proposal is said to be accepted. A proposal when accepted, becomes a promise." An agreement, therefore comes into existence only when one party makes a proposal or offer to the other party and that other party signifies his assent (i.e. gives his acceptance) thereto. In short, an agreement is the sum total of 'offer' and 'acceptance'.

Essential Elements of a Valid Contract

(a) **Offer and Acceptance**. There must be a "lawful offer" and a "lawful acceptance" of the offer. The term "lawful" implies that the offer and acceptance must satisfy the requirements of the Contract Act in relation thereto.

(b) **Intention to Create Legal Relations**. There must be an intention among the parties that the agreement should be attached by legal consequences and create obligations.

(c) **Lawful Consideration**. Consideration has been defined as the price paid by one party for the promise of the other. An agreement is legally enforceable only when each of the parties to it gives something and gets something. The something given or obtained is the price for the promise and is called 'consideration'.

(d) **Capacity of Parties**. The parties to an agreement must be competent to contract, otherwise it cannot be enforced by a court of law. In order to be competent to contract, the parties must be of the age of majority and of sound mind and must not be disqualified from contracting by any law to which they are subject (Section 11). If any of the parties to the agreement suffers from minority, lunacy, idiocy, drunkenness, etc, the agreement is not enforceable at law.

(e) **Free Consent**. There is absence of 'free consent', if the agreement is induced by (i) coercion (ii) undue influence (iii) fraud (iv) mis-representation or (v) mistake (Section 14). If the agreement is vitiated by any of the first four factors, the contract would be voidable and cannot be enforced by the party guilty of coercion, undue influence etc.

(f) **Lawful Object**. The object for which the agreement has been entered into must not be fraudulent or illegal or immoral or opposed to public policy or must not imply injury to the person or property of another (Section 23). If the object is unlawful for one or the other of the reasons mentioned above the agreement is void.

(g) **Writing and Registration**. Though an agreement may be oral or in writing, but in certain special cases to be valid must be in writing or registered.

(h) **Certainty**. An agreement, the maning of which is not certain or capable of being made certain are void.

(j) **Possibility of Performance**. An agreement to do an act impossible in itself is void.

(k) **Not expressly declared void**. The agreement must not have been expressly declared to be void under the Act.

Kinds of Contract from point of view of Enforceability

(a) **Valid Contract**. A valid contract is an agreement enforceable by law. An agreement becomes enforceable by law when all the essential elements of a valid contract as enumerated above are present.

(b) **Voidable Contract**. According to Section 2(I), "an agreement which is enforceable by law at the option of one or more of the parties thereto, but not at the option of the other or others, is a voidable contract." Thus, a voidable contract is one which is enforceable by law at the option of one of the parties. Until it is avoided or rescinded by the party entitled to do so by exercising his option in that behalf, it is a valid contract.

(c) **Void Contract**. The term 'void contract' implies a useless contract which has no legal effect at all, Such a contract is nullity as for there has been no contract at all.

(d) **Void Agreement**. An agreement not enforceable by law is said to be void" {Section 2(g)}. Thus, a void agreement does not give rise to any legal consequences and is void ab-initio. In the eye of law such an agreement is no agreement at all from its very inception.

(e) **Unenforceable Contract**. An unenforceable contract is one which is valid in itself, but is not capable of being enforced in a court of law because of some technical defect such as absence of writing, registration, requisite stamp, etc or time barred by the law of limitation.

(f) **Illegal or Unlawful Contract**. An agreement is illegal and void if its object or consideration: (i) is forbidden by law; or (ii) is of such a nature that, if permitted, it would defeat the provisions of any law; or (iii) is fraudulent; or (iv) involves or implies injury to the person or property of another; or (v) the court regards it as immoral or opposed to public policy (Section 23).

Kinds of Contracts from the Point of View of Mode of Creation

(a) **Express Contract.** Where both the offer and acceptance constituting an agreement enforceable at law are made in words spoken or written, is an express contract.

(b) **Implied Contract.** Where both the offer and acceptance constitu-ting an agreement enforceable at law are made otherwise than in words i.e. by acts and conduct of the parties, it is an implied contract.

Constructive or Quasi-Contract. The term 'constructive or quasi-contract' is a misnomer. The cases grouped under this type of contracts have little or no affinity with contract. Such a contract does not arise by virtue of any agreement, express or implied between the parties but the law infers or recognizes a contract under certain special circumstances.

Failure to honour a promise is not cheating. For instance, 'A' promises his girlfriend that he will marry her. Afterwards 'A' shifts his affection to another. A's girlfriend has not been cheated. But A will be liable for cheating if he promises his girlfriend marriage whilst all along not intending to fulfill it and causes her to either part with gifts or other valuables to him or enter into serious courtship and a physical relationship.

The Indian Partnership Act, 1932

"The most enlightened judicial policy is to let people manage their own business in their own way."

Oliver Wendell Holmes

Definition of "partnership", "partner", "firm" and "firm name". "Partnership" is the relation between persons who have agreed to share the profits of a business carried on by all or any of them acting for all (Section-4). The definition of partnership contains three elements—:

(a) There must be an agreement entered into by all the persons concerned.

(b) The agreement must be to share the profits of a business.

(c) The business must be carried on by all or any of the persons concerned acting for all.

Partnership not created by status. The relation partnership arises from contract and not from status.

Mode of determining existence of partnership. In determining whether a group of persons is or is not a firm, or whether a person is or is not a partner in a firm, regard shall be had to the real relationship between the parties, as shown by all relevant facts taken together (Section 6). The true test is whether such a participation of profits constitutes the relationship of principal and agent between the person taking the profits and those actually carrying on the business.

Partnership at will. Where no provision is made by contract between the partners for the duration of their partnership, or for the determination of their partnership, the partnership is 'partnership at will' (Section 7). A partnership at will is a partnership which can be dissolved at the instance of any of the partners.

General duties of partners. Partners are bound to carry on the business of the firm to the greatest common advantage, to be just and faithful to each other, and are to render true accounts and full information of all things affecting the firm to any partner or his legal representative (Section 9). All the partners are deemed to have such knowledge and notice of the acts of any of their partners relating to their business as in discharge of their plain duty they might or ought to have obtained.

The conduct of the business. Subject to contract between the partners (a) every partner has a right to take part in the conduct of business; (b) every partner is bound to attend diligently to his duties in the conduct of the business; (c) any difference arising as to ordinary matters connected with the business may be decided by a majority of the partners and every partner shall have the right to express his opinion before the matter is decided, but no change may be made in the nature of the business without the consent of all the partners; and (d) every partner has a right to have access to and to inspect and copy any of the books of the firm (Section 12).

The property of the firm. Subject to contract between the partners, the property of firm includes all property and rights and interests in property originally brought into the stock of the firm, or acquired, by purchase or otherwise, by or for the firm, or for the purposes and in the course of the business of the firm, and includes also the goodwill of the business (Section 14).

Application of the property of the firm. Subject to the contract between the partners, the property of the firm shall be held and used by the partners exclusively for the purposes of the business (Section 15). A partner would be an owner of the assets of the firm by virtue of this Section.

Partner to be agent of the firm. Subject to the provisions of this Act, a partner is the agent of the firm for the purposes of the business of the firm (Section 18).

Liability of a partner for acts of the firm. According to Section 25, every partner is liable, jointly with all the other partners and also severally, for all acts of the firm done while he is a partner. Partner is always liable for partnership debt unless there is implied or express restriction.

Introduction of a partner. Subject to contract between the partners and to the provisions of Section 30, no person shall be introduced as a partner in a firm without the consent of all the existing partners (Section 31).

Retirement of a partner. A partner may retire (a) with the consent of all the other partners, (b) in accordance with an express agreement by the partners, or (c) where the partnership is at Will, by giving notice in writing to all the other partners of his intention to retire (Section 32). Retirement of a partner with the consent of all the other partners can be effected without dissolution under this clause.

Expulsion of a partner. According to Section 33, a partner may not be expelled from a firm by any majority of the partners, save in the exercise in good faith of powers conferred by contract between the partners. The firm is bound by the transactions of the expelled partners with third parties until public notice of such expulsion is given.

Dissolution by agreement. According to Section 40, a firm may be dissolved with the consent of all the partners or in accordance with a contract between the partners. There is no dissolution of partnership firm by the mere incoming or outgoing of partners unless the contract between the partners so provides.

Liability for acts of partners done after dissolution. Notwithstanding the dissolution of a firm, the partners continue to be liable as such to third parties for any act done by any of them which would have been an act of the firm if done before the dissolution, until public notice is given of the dissolution.

Provided that the estate of a partner who dies, or who is adjudicated an insolvent, or of a partner who, not having been known to the person dealing with the firm to be a partner, retires from the firm, is not liable under this Section for acts done after the date on which he ceases to be a partner (Section 45).

This Section cannot be applied to the case of a debt owned by the partner in his individual capacity to his own creditors as distinct from the firms liability to the creditors of the firm.

Company Law

"It must be remembered that all trade is and must be in a sense selfish."

John Duke Coleridge

The Companies Act, 1956

The object sof the Act is to consolidate and amend the law relating to companies and certain other associations.

Company. Means a company formed and registered under this Act or an existing company as defined in clause (ii).

Private Company. Means a company which has a minimum paid-up capital of one lakh rupees or such higher paid-up capital as may be prescribed, and by its articles,

(a) restricts the right to transfer its shares, if any;

(b) limits the number of its members to fifty not including–

(i) persons who are in the employment of the company, and

(ii) persons who, having been formerly in the employment of the company, were members of the company while in that employment and have continued to be members after the employment ceased; and

(c) prohibits any invitation to the public to subscribe for any shares in, or debentures of, the company;

(d) prohibits any invitation or acceptance of deposits from persons other than its members, directors or their relatives.

Provided that where two or more persons hold one or more shares in a company jointly, they shall or the purposes of this definition, be treated as a single member;

Public Company. Means a company which (a) is not a private company; (b) has a minimum paid-up capital of five lakh rupees or such higher paid-up capital, as may be prescribed; and (c) is a private company which is subsidiary of a company which is not a private company.

Memorandum of Association. The memorandum of every company shall state its name, the state in which the registered office of the company is to be situated; its objects, any seven or more persons by subscribing their names to it and otherwise complying with the requirements of the Act, form an incorporated company, with or without limited liability.

Alternation of memorandum. A company shall not alter the conditions contained in its memorandum except in the cases, in the mode, and to the extent for which express provision is made in this Act.

Member. Any person who agrees in writing to become a member of a company and whose name is entered in its register of members, shall be a member of the company.

Prospectus. It is a document containing a statement of the property, business-undertaking, enterprise or project for the formation and development of a company for which an appeal is made to the public to subscribe for shares (Section 56). The requirement about registration of prospectus are contained in Section 50.

Nature of Shares or Debentures. The shares or debentures, other interest of any member in a company shall be movable property, transferable in the manner provided by the articles of the company.

Numbering of shares. Each share in a company having a share capital shall be distinguished by its appropriate number.

Certificate of shares. A certificate, under the common seal of the company, specifying any shares held by any member, shall be prima-facie evidence of the title of the member to such shares. Preference share capital and equity share capital are the two kinds of share capital. Every member of a company limited by shares and holding any equity share capital therein shall have a right to vote, in respect of such capital on every resolution place before the company; and his voting right on a poll shall be in proportion to his share of the paid up equity capital of the company.

Registered Office. A company shall, as from the day on which it begins to carry on business, or as from the 30th day after the date of its incorporation, whichever is earlier, have a registered office to which all communications or notices may be addressed.

Register of Members. Every company shall keep in one or more books a register of its members.

Meetings and Proceedings. The Act envisages following type of meetings.

(a) Statutory Meeting.

(b) Annual General Meeting.

(c) Extra-ordinary General Meeting

The provisions relating to notice quorum, chairman, proxies voting, poll, circulation of members resolution and minutes etc are contained in Section 171 to 197 of the Act.

The ordinary meaning of dividend is the receipt by the shareholder by reason of his being shareholder of part of the profits of the company of which he is a shareholder.

The Act also covers aspects pertaining to dividends, accounts audit, investigation, directors managing agents, powers of the Central Government, winding up etc.

The Sale Of Goods Act, 1930

"No pain, no palm; no thorns, no throne; no gall, no glory; no cross, no crown."

-Penn

The Sale of Goods Act, 1930, deals with law relating to the sale of goods. It appertains mainly to mercantile transactions. The under mentioned definitions are included in Section 2:-

"buyer" means a person who buys or agrees to buy goods. {Section 2(1)}

"delivery" means voluntary transfer of possession from one person to another. {Section 2(2)}

"goods" means every kind of movable property other than actionable claims and money; and inludes stock and shares, growing crops, grass, and things attached to or forming part of the land which are agreed to be severed before sale or under the contract of sale {Section 2(7)}. A railway receipt is a document of title.

"price" means a money consideration for a sale of goods {Section2(10)}. Normal price is the amount paid by the buyer for the purchase of goods.

"seller" means person who sells or agrees to sell goods. {Section 2(13)}

Sale and agreement to sell –A contract of sale of goods is a contract whereby the seller transfers or agrees to transfer the property in goods to the buyer for a price. There may be a contract of sale between one part-owner and another. {Section 4(1)}

Contract of sale how made? A contract of sale is made by an offer to buy or sell goods for a price and the acceptance of such offer. The contract may provide for the immediate delivery of the goods or immediate payment of the price or both, or for the delivery or payment by installments, or that the delivery or payment or both shall be postponed {Section 5(1)}. A contract of sale can be made by mere offer and acceptance. Neither payment nor delivery is necessary for the purpose.

Ascertainment of price. The price in a contract of sale may be fixed by the contract or may be left to be fixed in a manner thereby agreed or may be determined by the course of dealing between the parties. {Section 9(1)}

Sale by sample. A contract of sale is a contract for sale by same where there is a term in the contract, express or implied, to that effect. {Section 17(1)}

(a) that the bulk shall correspond with the same in quality.

(b) that the buyer shall have a reasonable opportunity of comparing the bulk with the sample;

(c) that the goods shall be free from any defect, rendering them un-merchantable, which would not be apparent on the reasonable examination of the sample. {Section 17(2)}

Duties of seller and buyer. It is the duty of the seller to deliver the goods and of the buyer to accept and pay for them, in accordance with the terms of the contract of sale. {Section 31}

Payment and delivery are concurrent conditions. Unless otherwise agreed, delivery of the goods and payment of the price are concurrent conditions, that is to say, the seller shall be ready and willing to give possession of the goods to the buyer in exchange for the price, and the buyer shall be ready to pay the price in exchange for possession of the goods. {Section 32)

Delivery. Delivery of goods sold may be made by doing anything which the parties shall agree be treated as delivery or which has the effect of putting the goods in the possession of the buyer or of any person authorized to hold them on his behalf. {Section 33}

Effect of part delivery. A delivery of part of goods in progress of the delivery of the whole has the same effect, for the purpose of passing the property in such goods, as a delivery of the whole; but a delivery of part of the goods, with an intention of severing it from the whole, does not operate as the delivery of remainder. {Section 34}

Damages for non-acceptance. Where the buyer wrongfully neglects or refuses to accept and pay for the goods, the seller may sue him for damages for non-acceptance. {Section 56}

Damages for non-delivery. Where the seller wrongfully neglects or refuses to deliver the goods to the buyer, the buyer may sue the seller for damages for non-delivery. {Section 57}

Transfer Of Property Act, 1882

Transfer of Property refers to an act by which a living person conveys property, in present or in future, to one or more other living persons or to himself and one or more other living persons; and "to transfer property" is to perform such an act.

Objects. The main objects of the Act are –

(1) to lay down uniform rules for transfer property; and

(2) to complete the code of contract law so far as it relates to immovable property.

Transfer. The term implies conveyance of property by a person entitled to it to a person having no title in it.

Immovable property. This includes land, benefits to arise out of land, things attached to the earth or permanently fastened to anything attached to the earth.

Essentials of a Valid Transfer

1. The property must be transferable.
2. The transferor must be competent to transfer.
3. The transferee must be competent to take the transfer.
4. The consideration and the object of the transfer must be lawful.
5. The transfer must not be opposed to the nature of interest affected thereby.
6. The transfer must be made in the manner and form prescribed by the Act, if any.

Alienation

Alienation means conveyance of transfer of property to another. Public policy requires that property should be freely alienable. A right alienation is incidental to and inseparable from the beneficial ownership of property.

Restraint on alienation may be –

(a) Absolute, or

(b) Partial

Vested Interest. To vest means to clothe with legal rights. An interest is said to be vested in possession when it gives a present right to the transferee to the immediate possession or enjoyment of property.

Contingent Interest. Where, on a transfer of property, an interest therein is created in favour of a person to take effect only on the happening of a specified uncertain event, or if a specified uncertain event shall not happen, such person, thereby, acquires a contingent interest in property.

Sale. Sale is a transfer of ownership in exchange for a price paid or promised or part-paid and part-promised.

Mode of Sale

1. By registered instrument.
2. By delivery of possession.

Seller's Liabilities before the Completion of Sale

1. Disclosure of material defects.
2. Production of title deeds.
3. Duty to answer questions.
4. Execution of conveyance.
5. Reasonable care of property.
6. Payment of charge.

After completion of Sale

1. Delivery of possession.
2. Implied covenant of title.
3. Delivery of title deeds.

Buyer's Liabilities Before Completion of Sale

1. Duty to disclose facts.
2. Duty to tender price.

After completion of Sale

1. Duty to bear loss.
2. Duty to pay public charges and rent.

Mortgage. A mortgage is the transfer of an interest in specific immovable property for the purpose of securing the payment of money advanced or to be advanced by way of loan, an existing or future debt, or the performance of an engagement which may give rise to a pecuniary liability.

The transferor is called a mortgagor, the transferee a mortgagee; the principal money and interest of which payment is secured for the time being are called the mortgage money, and the instrument (if any) by which the transfer is effected is called a mortgage-deed.

Characteristics of a Mortgage

1. Writing and registration.
2. Transfer of interest in specific immovable property.
3. Transfer of interest by way of security.
4. Sale of subject matter.
5. Interest re-conveyed.

Mortgage and Pledge

The important points of difference are –

	Mortgage	Pledge
1	It relates to immovable property.	I relates to movable property.
2	There is a transfer of interest in some specific immovable property.	There is only obligation to repay money.
3	The property in which mortgage is created may or may not be transferred to the mortgagee.	The possession of property which is pledged is handed over to the creditor (pledgee).
4	There is no bar on creating a number of mortgages on one property.	This is not possible in case of Pledge.

Right of Mortgagor

1. Right of redemption.
2. Right of assigning the mortgage instead of re-transfer.
3. Right to inspection and production of documents.
4. Right to redeem separately or simultaneously.
5. Right of usufructuary mortgagor to recover possession.
6. Right to accession to mortgaged property.
7. Right to improvement to mortgaged property.
8. Benefit of new lease.
9. Power to make lease.

Liabilitics of Mortgagor

1. Covenant for title.
2. Covenant for defence of title.
3. Covenant for payment of public charges.
4. Covenant where the mortgaged property is a lease.
5. Covenant for payment of prior incumbrances.
6. Right tin case of renewal of mortgaged lease.
7. Right to spend money.
8. Right to proceeds of revenue, sale or compensation on acquisition.

Charges. Where immovable property of one person is by act of parties or operation of law made security for the payment of money to another, and the transaction does not amount to a mortgage, the latter person is said to have a charge on the property; and all the provisions hereinbefore contained which apply to a simple mortgage shall, so far as may be, apply to such charge.

Lease. A lease of immovable property is a transfer of a right to enjoy such property, made for a certain time, express or implied, or in perpetuity, in consideration of a price paid or promised, or of money, a share of crops, service or any other thing of value, to be rendered periodically or on specified occasions to the transferor by the transferee, who accepts the transfer on such terms.

Essentials of a lease

1. Transfer.
2. Right to enjoy.
3. Duration.
4. Consideration.
5. Acceptance by the transferee.

Exchange

When two persons mutually transfer the ownership of one thing for the ownership of another, neither thing, or both things being money only, the transaction is called an "exchange".

A transfer of property in completion of an exchange can be made only in manner provided for the transfer of such property by sale.

Gift

"Gift" is the transfer of certain existing movable or immovable property made voluntarily and without consideration, by one person, called the donor, to another, called the donee, and accepted by or on behalf of the donee.

Essenitals of Gift

1. Transfer of ownership.
2. Property must be in existence.
3. Voluntary transfer.
4. Without Consideration.
5. Acceptance by the donee.

Section 52 of the Transfer of Property Act enacts the doctrine of '**lis pendens**'. Put simply, it means any right to immovable property, which is the subject matter of a legal proceeding, cannot be transferred or dealt with so as to defeat the rights of any party to the suit, except under the order of the court that is hearing the proceeding. This is necessary because otherwise, the plaintiff's right in every such suit would be defeated by reason of the defendant transferring before the judgement or decree. The plaintiff would then have to file another suit against the new purchaser, and repeat the process indefinitely, because every defendant would sell to a new purchaser before the judgement or decree. Thus, the plaintiff would never be able to succeed in his suit.

Labour Laws

"No abilities, however splendid, can command success without intense labour and preserving application."

AT Stewart

The Workmen Compensation Act, 1923

The above Act grants a statutory right to the workers to recover compensation for injury caused by accident arising out of and in course of employment. Such measure has to be construed giving the widest scope to the ameliorative and beneficial provision intended by the legislation.

Dependent. In relation to a deceased workman the terms means a widow, minor legitimate son, an unmarried legitimate daughter or a widowed mother etc. Right Of Dependent to get compensation accrues on the date of death of the workman.

Employer. The definition includes any body of persons whether incorporated or not, any managing agent etc.

Workman. The term defines a railway servant or any person who is employed in any such capacity as is specified in Schedule 2 in Chapter 7 of the Act. This does not include members of the Armed Forces.

Wages. The term is defined to include any privilege or benefit which is capable of being estimated in money. This does not include travelling allowances.

Disablement. The Act defines partial and total disablement. These definitions clearly show that "disablement" is a loss of earning capacity, which depending on the nature of injury and percentage of loss of earning capacity, can be partial or total. The Act classifies "disablement" into two categories, namely Partial Disablement and Total Disablement.

Basis of Liability {Section 3}. Liability can be assessed in the following three manners.

(a) Employer's Liability. If personal injury is caused to a workman by accident arising out of and in the course of his employment, his employer is liable to pay compensation in accordance with the provisions of Sections 3 to 18A of the Act.

(b) Occupation Diseases. As compensation is payable under the Act on account of injury arising out of accident. It was considered necessary to specify that occupational diseases are to be regarded as injuries arising out of accident. It was essential to clarify this as ordinarily a disease is not included in the concept of 'injury arising out of accident'. Insanity and allied disorders are not to be found in occupational diseases.

(c) Bar to Claim. Under Section 3(5), a claim for compensation under the Act is barred inter alia by a prior civil suit for damages on account of the inquiry. There must be a casual relationship between the accident and the employment. Compensation matters are always civil matters and like all civil matters they are to be decided on the basis of preponderance of probability.

Amount of Compensation {Section-4}. The provisions relating to the quantum of compensation are contained in Section 4. These provisions may be divided into separate contingencies contemplated by the section.:

(a) Death.

(b) Permanent Total Disablement.

(c) Permanent PartialDisablement; and

(d) Temporary Disablement – whether partial or total.

The period during which loss of earning capacity was not actually suffered, if at all does not come into picture at all.

Employer's Obligations. This is discussed under the following five heads;

(a) Statement regarding fatal accidents (Section 10A).

(b) Reports of fatal accidents and serious bodily injuries (Section 10B).

(c) Returns regarding compensation (Section 16).

(d) Contracting out (Section 17).

(e) Penalities (Section 18A).

This Act is a piece of social secuiity legislation interpretation of which would advance salutary object and intendment of the Act should be adopted. It cannot be interpreted too narrowly so as to debar a workman from compensation which the Parliament thought they ought to have.

If you know how much you've got, you probably hav'nt got much.

Imelda Marcos

The Payment of Wages Act, 1936

The right of workmen to receive their wages in a particular manner, at specified times, and without any unauthorized deduction, has been granted by the Payment of Wages Act, 1936. The Act, therefore, is a weapon in the hands of the workmen to ensure that in matters relating to wage payment and deductions there from, the employers conduct is governed by the provisions of law. It enables a speedy recovery of wages by the use of the machinery under the Act, and spares the employed person from the trouble and expense of having to take recourse in ordinary Civil Court.

The Act applies to persons employed in any factory, upon any railway, and employed in an industrial or other establishment. The person should be employed in the premises of a factory. He need not be working in the manufacturing process.

Wages. The term has been defined to mean payment of remuneration whether by salary, allowance or otherwise. The definition is exhaustive in the sense that it indicates what has to be included and what has to be excluded.

Responsibility for Wage Payment (Section 3). The liability for the payment of wages is fixed by Section 3, which lays down that every employer is responsible for the payment to persons employed by him of all wages required to be paid under the Act. Responsibility for payment of wages is that of the manager where one such is appointed.

Fixation of Wage Periods (Section 4). Under Section 4, every person responsible for the payment of wages under Section 3, must fix wage periods in respect of which such wages are payable. No wage period can, however, exceed one month. The word 'wage' as used in the statute must be construed to mean 'earned wage' as distinguished from potential wages.

Time for Wage Payment (Section 50). The provisions of Section 5, which deal with the time for the payment of wages, may be analysed as follows:

(a) *Time for Payment.* Wages of every employed person must be paid within the time mentioned in Section 5 in the time frame indicated for employment in a factory, railway or other industrial establishment or dock, mine etc.

(b) In the situation of termination of employment, it is to be paid before expiry of second working day from the date of termination.

Mode of Payment (Section 6). This Section provides that all wages are to be paid in current coins or currency notes, or in both. However, if the employer has obtained the written authorization of the employed person, he may pay him such wages either by the cheque, or by crediting the wages to his bank account. (Provision to Section 6)

Maintenance of Registers (Section 13A). Section 13A casts a duty on the employer in respect of the maintenance of registers and records. According to this section, the employer must :

(a) Maintain the prescribed registers and records in the prescribed form which provide the following particulars.

   (i) Persons employed.

   (ii) Work performed by them.

   (iii) Wage paid to them.

   (iv) Deductions made from their wages.

   (v) The receipts given by them, etc.

(b) Have the register and record preserved for a period of three years after the date of the last entry made therein.

The Negotiable Instruments Act, 1881

"Money speaks sense in a language all nations understand."

Aphra Behn

A negotiable instrument may be dishonoured by

(i) non-acceptance; or

(ii) non-payment.

Promissory Note. A "promissory note" is an instrument in writing (not being a bank-note or a currency note) containing an unconditional undertaking, signed by the maker, to pay a certain sum of money only to, or to the order of, a certain person, or to the bearer of the instrument.

Bill of Exchange. A "bill of exchange" is an instrument in writing containing an unconditional order, signed by the maker, directing a certain person to pay a certain sum of money only to, or to the order of, a certain person or to the bearer of the instrument.

Cheque. A "cheque" is a bill of exchange drawn on a specified banker and not expressed to be payable otherwise than on demand.

Drawer "Drawee". The maker of a bill of exchange or cheque is called the "drawer", the person, thereby, directed to pay is called the "drawee".

Acceptor. After the drawee of a bill has signed his assent upon the bill, or, if there are more parts thereof than one, upon one of such parts, and delivered the same, or given notice of such signing to the holder or to some person on his behalf, he is called the "acceptor".

Payee. The person named in the instrument, to whom or to whose order the money is by the instrument directed to be paid, is called the "payee".

Holder. The "holder" of a promissory note, bill of exchange or cheque means any person entitled in his own name to the possession thereof and to receive or recover the amount due thereon from the parties thereto. (Section 8)

Holder in due courses. "Holder in due course" means any person who for consideration became the possessor of a promissory note, bill of exchange or cheque if payable to bearer. (Section 9)

A promissory note, bill of exchange or cheque which is

(i) Drawn or made in India and also made payable in India, or

(ii) Drawn or made in India upon any person resident in India, although it may be made payable in a foreign country, is deemed to be an inland instrument. (Section 11)

An instrument, which is not an inland instrument, is deemed to be a foreign instrument.

Negotiable Instrument. "Negotiable instrument" means a promissory note, bill of exchange or cheque payable either to order or to bear.(Section 13)

Negotiation. When a promissory note, bill of exchange or cheque is transferred to any person, so as to constitute the person the holder thereof, the instrument is said to be negotiated. (Section 14)

Indorsement. When the maker or holder of negotiable instrument signs the same, otherwise than as such maker, for the purpose of negotiation, on the back or face thereof or on a slip of paper annexed thereto, or so signs for the same purpose a stamped paper intended to be completed as a negotiable instrument, he is said to indorse the same, and is called the "indorser".(Section 15)

Capacity to make, etc promissory notes, etc. Every person capable of contracting, according to the law to which he is subject, may bind himself and be bound by the making, drawing, acceptance, indorsement, delivery and negotiation of a promissory note, bill of exchange or cheque. (Section-26)

Liability of drawer. The drawer of bill of exchange or cheque is bound in case of dishonour by the drawee or acceptor thereof, to compensate the holder, provided due notice of dishonour has been given to, or received by, the drawer as hereinafter provided. As soon as a negotiable instrument is dishonoured (either by non-acceptance or by non-payment) the holder becomes entitled to sue the parties liable to pay thereon.

Liability of draw of cheque. The drawee of a cheque having sufficient funds of the drawer in his hands properly applicable to the payment,such cheque must pay the cheque when duly required so to do, and, in default of such payment, must compensate the drawer for any loss or damage caused by such default. (Section 31)

Delivery. The making, acceptance or indorsement of a promissory note, bill of exchange or cheque is completed by delivery, actual or constructive. (Section 46)

Negotiation by delivery. Subject to the provisions of Section 58, a promissory note, bill of exchange or cheque payable to bearer is negotiable by delivery thereof. (Section 47)

Effect of indorsement. The indorsement of a negotiable instrument followed by delivery transfers to indorsee the property therein with the right of further negotiation; but the indorsement may by express words, restrict or exclude such right, or may merely constitute the indorsee an agent to indorse the instrument, or to receive its contents for the indorser, or for some other specified person. (Section 50)

Drawee's time for deliberation. The holder must, if so required by the drawee of a bill of exchange presented to him for acceptance, allow the drawee forty eight hours (exclusive public holidays) to consider whether he will accept it. (Section 63) A bill of exchange is said to be dishonoured by non-acceptance in various manners eg. Sections 61,63 or 115 etc.

Notice of dishonour means formal communication of the fact of dishonour.

Presentment for payment. Promissory notes, bills of exchange and cheques must be present for payment to the maker, acceptor, or drawee thereof respectively, by or on behalf of the holder as hereinafter provided. In default of such presentment, the other parties thereto are not liable thereon to such holder. (Section 64)

Notice of dishonour must be given by the holder or by some party to the instrument who remains liable thereon. (Section 93)

Notice of dishonour must be given to all parties (other than the maker of a note, acceptor of a bill or drawee of a cheque) to whom the holder seeks to make liable or to their duly authorized agents.

Consequence of not giving notice of dishonour is that the party is discharged from his obligation under the instrument and cannot be sued by the holder.

Cheque crossed generally. Where a cheque bears across its face an addition of the words "and company" or any abbreviation thereof, between two parallel transverse lines, or of two parallel transverse lines imply, either with or without the words "not negotiable", that addition shall be deemed a crossing, and the cheque shall be deemed to be crossed generally. (Section 123)

Taxation

"Money is not the measure of a man, but it is often the means of finding out how small he is."

–Disraeli

The ideology of taxation is broadly based on three basic considerations –to raise revenue, to bring about certain economic and social results and to discourage consumption and use of articles which the State regards as obnoxious.

According to Adam Smith, four main objectives should be borne in mind by the State in levying taxes, Firstly, equity. The taxes must be equitable and fair as between different classes of society. Secondly, the convenience of the tax payer. Taxes must not be so complicated and so 'cumbersome in their operation as to cause needless inconvenience and hardships to the people. Thirdly, economy. The Government must economize and levy only the minimum tax which is necessary for the national good. Fourthly, certainty and clarity. The laws imposing taxes must be so precisely and clearly worded as to make the tax payer understand what exactly is the burden he is called upon to bear.

The canons of taxation in modern times have been stated to be–social justice, constancy with economic goals, ease of administration and compliance and revenue adequacy.

Income Tax is of three types (i) progressive tax, where the rate increases with the higher slabs of income, (ii) proportional, where the rate remains constant at all levels of income; and (iii) regressive, where the rate comes down as one approaches higher slabs of income.

Income Tax Act, 1961

Taxes are the life-blood of any Government. Every Government has a right to levy taxes. The Income Tax Act, 1961 is a complex and voluminous piece of legislation. Over the years, it has undergone scores of amendments. According to Nani Palkhivala, "There is no other instance in Indian jurisprudence of an Act mutilated by more than 3300 amendments in less than 30 years." Its text runs into 298 sections and 14 schedules. The contents have been grouped under 23 chapters.

The scheme of the Act explains the basis of charge and incomes which do not form part of total income. Extensive provisions have been framed concerning computation of total income from different heads (Chapter IV). The statute addresses itself to income of other persons included in assessee's total income (Chapter V), aggregation of income and set off for carry forward of loss (Chapter VI) and deductions to be made in computing total income (Chapter VIA). Rebates and reliefs (Chapter VIII), double taxation relief (Chapter IX) and special provisions relating to avoidance of tax (Chapter X) have also been taken into account.

The other matters relate to

		Chapter
1.	Determination of tax in certain special cases	XII
2.	Special Provisions Relating to certain Incomes of Non Residents	XIIA
3.	Special Provision	XIIB to F
4.	Income Tax Authorities	XIII
5.	Procedure for Assessment	XIV
6.	Search Cases	XIVB
7.	Liability in Special Cases	XV
8.	Collection & Recovery of Tax	XVII
9.	Refunds	XIX
10.	Settlement of Cases	XIXA
11.	Appeals and Revision	XX
12.	Penalties Imposable	XXI
13.	Offences and Prosecution	XXII

Definitions

Assessment Year It means a period of twelve months, commencing on the 1st day of April every year.

Books or Books of Account. Include ledgers, day books, cash books, account books and other books, whether kept in the written form or as print outs of data stored in a floopy disc, tape or any other form of electro magnetic data storage device.

Business. Includes any trade, commerce or manufacture or any adventure or concern in the nature of trade, commerce or manufacture.

Company. It means any Indian company or any body corporate incorporated by or under the laws of a country outside India.

Domestic Company. It means an Indian company, or any other company which, in respect of its income liable to tax under this Act, has made the prescribed arrangements for the declaration and payment, within India, of the dividends (including dividends or preference shares), payable out of such income;

Previous Year. The financial year immediately preceding the assessment year.

Heads of Income. Save as otherwise provided by this Act, all income shall, for the purposes of charge of income-tax and computation of total income, be classified under the following heads of income:

(a) Salaries.

(b) Income from house property.

(c) Profits and gains of business or profession.

(d) Capital gains.

(e) Income from other sources.

Development Rebate. In respect of a new ship or new machinery or plaint (other than office appliances or road transport vehicles) which is owned by the assessee and is wholly used for the purposes of the business carried on by him, there shall, in accordance with and subject to the provisions of this section and of section 34, be allowed a deduction, in respect of the previous year in which the ship was acquired or the machinery or plant was installed or, if the ship, machinery or plant is first put to use in the immediately succeeding previous year, then, in respect of that previous year, a sum by way of development rebate as specified in clause (b).

Development Allowances. In respect of planting of tea bushes on any land in India owned by an assessee who carries on business of growing and manufacturing tea in India, a sum by way of development allowance equivalent to–

(a) Where tea bushes have been planted on any land not planted at any time with tea bushes or on any land which had been previously abandoned, 50 per cent of the actual cost of planting; and

(b) Where tea bushes are planted in replacement of tea bushes that have died or have become permanently useless on any land already planted, 30 per cent of the actual cost of planting.

The survey involves an element of surprise to unearth/ detect evasion of tax. Income tax authority can survey any place within the limits of the area assigned to him or any place where he exercises jurisdiction or a place where he is authorized. Survey can be carried out at premises where business or profession is carried out.

Industrial Law

"Strong responsible unions are essential to industrial fair play. Without them the labour bargain is wholly one-sided."

Louis D Brandeis

The object of the industrial law is two-fold, namely, (i) to improve the service conditions of industrial labour so as to provide for them the ordinary amenities of life and (ii) by that process to bring about industrial peace which would in its turn accelerate productive activity of the country resulting in its prosperity.

Industrial Disputes Act, 1947

This Statute was enacted to make provisions for the investigation and settlement of industrial disputes. It is calculated to ensure social justice to both employers and employees and advance the progress of industry by bringing about the existence of harmony and cordial relations between the parties. Scope and effect of the Act is to promote industrial peace, legitimate trade union activities and discouragement of improper or unfair employer practices or victimization of workers.

Definitions

Award. It means an interim or a dinal determination of any industrial disputer or of any question relating thereto by any Labour Court, Industrial Tribunal or National Industrial Tribunal and includes an arbitration award made under Section 10A. {section 2(b)}. An award is not in the nature of interim relief for it decides the industrial dispute or some question relating thereto.

Closure. It means the permanent closing down of a place of employment or part thereof. {Section 2(c)}. Mere change of ownership of factory would not amount to an act of closure of factory.

Executive. In relation to a trade union, means the body by whatever name called to which the management of the affairs of the trade union is entrusted. {Section 2(gg)}

Industrial Dispute. It means any dispute or difference between employers and employees or between employers and workmen, which is connected with the employment or non-employment or the terms of employment or with the conditions of labour, of any person. {Section 2(k)}. The defination of "industrial dispute" is in three parts. The first part refers to the factum of a real and substantial dispute. The second part to the dispute and the third to the subject matter of the dispute.

Lay off. It means the failure, refusal or inablility of an employer on account of shortage of coal, power or raw materials or the accumulation of stocks or the break-down of machinery or natural calamity or for any other connected reason to give employment to a workman whose name is borne on the muster rolls of his industrial establishments and who has not been retrenched. {Section 2(kkk)}. The defination is general and would apply when an employer did not or could not, because of the circumstances specified in the section, give emploument to a worlman.

Lock out. Temprar closing of a place of employment or the suspension od work, or the redusal by an employer to continue to employ any number of persons employed by him. {Section 2(i)}. A lock out is distinct and different from a closure of business even temporarily. In the case of lockout the industry as such is not closed down even temporarily.

Retrenchment. It means the termination by the employer of the service of a workman for any reason whatsoever, otherwise than as a punishment inflicted by way of disciplinary action. {Section 2(oo)}. The definition does specifically include the case either or transfer of business or of a closure of an industry.

Settlement. It means a settlement arrived at in the course of concilliation proceeding and includes a written agreement between the employer and workmen arrived at otherwise than in the course of concilliation proceeding where such agreement has been signed by the parties thereto in such manner as may be prescribed and a copy there of has been sent to the authority of the appropriater Government and the concilliation officer {Section 2(p)}. The term necessitates the investigation of facts before it is decided that it was a settlement.

Strike. It means a cessation of work by a body of persons employed in any industry acting in combination or a concerted refusal, or a refusal under a common understanding, of any number of persons who are or have been so employed to continue to work or to accept employment. {Section 2(a)}. Cessation of work even for a hours as a result of the concerted action of the workers amounts to a strike.

Under Section 2A even an industrial dispute arising out of discharge, dismissal, retrenchment or termination, is an industrial dispute not with standing that no other workman or any union of workmen is a party to the dispute.

Section 3 of the Act empowers the appropriate Government to constitute Works Committee in industrial establishment employing hundred or more workmen. Such Works Committee shall have representative both of employer and their workmen. The number of the representative of the workmen shall not be less than those of the employer.

The representatives of the workmen are required to be chosen in the manner prescribed by the rules, from among the workmen engaged in the establishment and in consultation with their registered trade union, if any.

The duty of the Works Committee is to promote measures for securing and preserving amity and good relations between the employees and the workmen with regard to matters of their common interest and to comment on such matters. Where the Works Committee fails to settle the disputes arising between the employer and his workmen, services of Conciliation Officers and Boards of Concilliation may be taken to assist the parties to settle their disputes.

During July 2003, the Supreme Court of India in one of its judgements denied workers the right to strike. It imposed a constraint on workers collective right to strike. The court seems to be of the opinion that the machinery avaible for collective bargaining, consultation, conciliation and arbitration is sufficient to avoid the need for strikes.

Courts of Inquiry. The appropriate Government may as occasion arises by notification in the Official Gazette constitute a court of Inquiry for industrial dispute (Section 6). The word 'court' as used in the Act would not mean the civil court or any other court.

Labour Courts. Empowers the appropriate Government to constitute Labour Court for adjudication of industrial disputes relating to matters mentioned in Section 7. Schedule Labour Court may also be assigned to perform other functions. A Labour Court shall consist of a single person appointed by the appropriate Government as its Presiding Officer.

Industrial Tribunal. Section 7A empowers the appropriate Government to constitute one or more Industrial Tribunals. The appointment of the Tribunals have been vested with powers wider than those of a Labour Court in as much as while the latter has jurisdiction to adjudicate matters specified in the Second Schedule and such other functions as may be assigned to it, the Industrial Tribunal can decide industrial disputes whether they fall in the Second or the Third Schedule.

Notice of Change. The provision of Section 9A lays down the procedure for bringing about a change in the conditions of service of the workmen in respect of matters specified in the Fourth Schedule appended to the Act. Before making any change in conditions of service of workmen, employer has a duty to give notice of it.

Section 10 of the Act empowered the appropriate Government by order in writing (i) to refer the dispute to a Tribunal for adjudication, or (ii) to refer any matter "appearing to be connected with or relevant to the dispute to a Court of Inquiry", when an industrial dispute existed or was apprehended. The function of a Tribunal was to adjudicate on the 'dispute' and make its award on the 'dispute' or 'any question relating thereto', and to make enquiry 'on matter appearing to be connected with or relevant to the dispute' and submit its report.

Voluntary Reference of Dispute to Arbitration. Section 10A has been enacted to provide for voluntary reference of disputes to arbitration to persons of their own choice by the parties themselves by written agreement at any time before the appropriate Government has referred such dispute under Section 10. It deals with what the parties agree and provides that if the parties agree and reduce their agreement to writing a reference shall be made to the person or persons named by such writing. The fact that the parties can agree to refer their dispute to the labour court, tribunal or national tribunal make no difference to the construction of the provision.

Prohibition of Strikes and Lock Outs. It prohibits workmen from going on strike and employers from locking out his workmen in converns dealing with a public utility service without giving notice as laid down in the section. The notice must be given within six weeks before striking or lockout. That is if a notice of strike or lock-out was given more than six weeks prior to the date of going on strike or locking out, it will not be deemed to comply the provisions of the section and will therefore render the strike or lock-out illegal. Strike or lock-out cannot be commenced within fourteen days of giving such notice or before expiry of the date strike specified in a any conciliation proceedings before the conciliation officer. It may, however, commence seven days after the conclusion of a conciliation proceeding. (Section 22).

Illegal Strikes and Lock Outs. Section 24 makes a strike or lock-out illegal if it is commenced or declared in contravention of the provisions of Section 22 or 23 of the Act or if it is continued where an industrial dispute had been referred to a Board, Arbitrator, Labour Court, Tribunal or National Tribunal and the appropriate Government has by order prohibited the continuance of the strike or lock-out in connection with such dispute which may be in existence on the date of the reference. Therefore strikes or lock-outs not commenced, declared or continued as aforesaid may be regarded as legal.

No person shall knowingly expend or apply any money in direct furtherance of support of any illegal strike or lock-out (Section 25) It is prohibited to give any financial aid to illegal strike and lock-outs. It does not mention that any help in kind would also fall within the purview of its provisions.

Lay off and Retrenchment. The Industrial Disputes Act provides as to when lay-off compensation should be awarded and the Tribunals have no jurisdiction to award such compensation in cases not governed by the Act. The stature cannot be circumvented by calling it "unemployment compendation" or by any other name. So compensation cannot be granted to the lay-off workmen on general principle laid down in cases of lay-off occurring prior to the enactment of Chapter V-A of the Act simply because an industrial establishment employs less than 50 workmen on an average per working day in any calendar month.

Section 25 C has been enacted to give a statutory recognition to the right of a workman to receive lay-off compensation. It provides that a workman who has completed not less than one year continuous or intermittently, shall be paid by the employer for the days during which he has been laid-off, compensation equal to 50 per cent his wages and dearness allowance payable to him for the period. In counting the number of the days for which the workman has been laid-off the weekly holidays shall have to be excluded.

Prohibition of Lay-Offs. Significantly enough, so far as production of figures, position of stock and sales figures are concerned, the management is expected to furnish month-wise information for 12 months preceding, the date of the application for permission. The whole endeavour, therefore, is expected to be ascertain whether on the date on which the lay-off is proposed to be given, the circumstances justifying the lay-off exist or not. Hence, it is incumbent on the management to commerce the lay-off from the date mentioned in the application or if the date has already expired, then from the date of the order. {Section 25(M)}

Unfair Labour Practice. No employer of workman or a trade union, whether registered under the Trade Unions Act, 1926, or not, shall commit any unfair labour practice (Section 25-T). The obligation not to transfer a workman malafide from one place to another under the guise of management policy was not recongnized under the common law. That right is now created by the Statute.

Penalty for illegal strikes and lock-outs. Any workman who commences, continues or otherwise acts in futherance of, a strike which is illegal under this Act, shall be punishable with imprisonment for a term which may extend to one month, or with fine which may extend to fifty rupees, or with both. Any employer who commences, continues, or otherwise acts in furtherance of lock-out which is illegal under this Act, shall be punishable with imprisonment for a term which may extend to one month, or with fine which may extend to one thousand rupees, or with both.

Note

6

Judicial Processes

"To be effective, judicial administration must not be leaden-footed."

Felix Frankfurter

Types of Writ

A writ is a judicial process by which a person is summoned to appear. It is a legal instrument to enforce obedience to the orders and sentences of the courts. Writs bear the seal of the crown or court. The Constitution of India makes a mention of the under mentioned five types of writs. These writs are issued as extra-ordinary remedies in cases where there was either no remedy available under the ordinary law or the remedy available was inadequate.

1. Habeas Corpus
2. Mandamus
3. Prohibition
4. Certiorari
5. Quo-warranto

Habeas Corpus

This writ is a remedy available to a person who is confined without legal justification to secure the release from his confinement. The writ is, in form, an order issued by the High Court calling upon the person by whom a person is alleged to be kept in confinement to bring such person before the court and to let the court know on what ground the person is confined. If there is no legal justification for the detention, the person is ordered to be released. It is the duty of the court to issue this writ to safeguard the freedom of the citizen against arbitrary and illegal detention. However, the production of the body of the person alleged to be unlawfully detained is essential before an application for a writ of habeas corpus can be finally heard and disposed of by the court. In Kanu Sanyal V DM, AIR 1973 SC 2684; Bhagwati, J held that the production of the body of the person alleged to be wrongfully detained is ancillary to the main purpose of the writ in securing the liberty of the subject illegally detained.

Subject to the rules framed by various High Courts an application for habeas corpus can be made by the person in confinement or by any other person on his behalf. Every application for a writ of habeas corpus has to be accompanied by an affidavit stating the nature and circumstances of the confinement. On an application for the writ the usual procedure is that if the court considers that a prima facie case for grating the prayer has been made out, it issues a *rule nisi* calling upon the opposite party to show cause, on a day specified, why an order granting the writ should not be made. On the day so specified that court considers the sufficiency of the cause shown (technically called the "return" to the writ of habeas corpus). If the cause shown in the return made by the jailor, or any person detaining the applicant, discloses that the detention is unjustified, the court will order immediate release of the detained person. This it does by making the *rule nisi* absolute which has the effect of setting the detenu free. If the detention is justified, the *rule nisi* shall be discharged.

A person has no right to present successive applications for habeas corpus to different judges of the same court. However, a fresh petition under Article 32 would be competent. The rule of English law is such that no appeal lies against an order of discharge of a person on habeas corpus. In India there is no such law and an appeal can lie to the Supreme Court under Article 132, 133,134 and 136 against an order granting and rejecting the application for issue of the writ.

Mandamus

The word 'Mandamus' literally means a command. The writ of mandamus is thus a command issued to direct any person, corporation, inferior court or government requiring him to do or forbear from doing some specific act which that body is obliged under law to do or refrain from doing, as the case may be, and which is in the nature of a public duty and in certain cases of a statutory duty. No one can ask for a mandamus without a legal right. There must be a judicially enforceable as well as legally protected right by someone who has a legal duty to do something and abstains from doing it.

No mandamus will lie where the duty is of a discretionary nature. For the same reason, no mandamus would lie to enforce administrative instruction without any statutory force since no right can be founded on such instructions. One of the conditions for the grant of the relief of mandamus is that there must a demand for the relief and its refusal by the authority concerned. In Naubat Rai V Union of India, AIR

1953 Punj 137, the petitioner, who was in the service of the Military Farms Department was removed from the service by the departmental head, he applied for a writ of mandamus. But it was not shown whether he had applied for reinstatement or had he even applied under the service rules against the order of removal and that such demand was denied. It was held that the application under Article 226 was denied. It was held that the application under Article 226 was not maintainable.

Certiorari

It is available to any person whenever any body of persons having legal authority to determine questions affecting the rights of subjects and having the duty to act judicially act in excess of their legal authority. The writ of certiorari is an order of the High Court issued to inferior courts, tribunals or authorities to transmit to it the record of proceeding pending with them for scrutiny and, if necessary, for quashing the same. In an often cited English case of R V Electricity Commissioner, Atkin, Lord Justice said the writ of certiorari may be issued "wherever any body of persons having legal authority to determine questions affecting the rights of subjects, and having the duty to act judicially, act in excess of their legal authority. Whenever any body or person:

(a) having legal authority

(b) to determine questions affecting the rights of subject

(c) having the duty to act judicially

(d) act in the exercise of their legal authority, a writ of certiorari may be issued. Unless all these conditions are fulfilled mere inconvenience or absence of other remedy does not create a right to certiorari.

The writ of certiorari can be issued to a judicial or quasi-judicial body on the following grounds:

(a) Want or excess of jurisdiction.

(b) Violation of procedure or disregard of principle of natural justice.

(c) Error of law apparent on the face of the record.

The court issuing a writ of certiorari acts in exercise of a supervisory and nor appellate jurisdiction. The consequence of this is that the court will not review findings of fact reached by the inferior court or tribunal even if they are erroneous. This is based on the principle that a court which has jurisdiction to decide wrongly as well as rightly and when the legislature does not choose to confer a right of appeal against decision, it would be defeating its purpose and policy, if a superior court were to rehear the case on the evidence and substitute its findings. The function of certiorari is to quash the offending order and not to substitute a new order in its place.

Quo-Warranto

The writ of quo warranto enables enquiry into the legality of the claim which a person asserts to an office or franchise and to oust him from such position if he is an usurper. The object of this writ is to prevent a person who has wrongfully usurped an office from continuing in that office. The writ calls upon the holder of the office to show to the court under what authority he holds the office. If the court determines that the incumbent is holding the office in question illegally, it would pass the order of ouster which must be obeyed by him. Before a citizen can claim a writ of quo-warranto, he must satisfy the court that the office in question is a public office and is held by an usurper without legal authority and that necessarily leads to the enquiry as to whether the appointment of the said alleged usurper has been made in accordance with law or not. The conditions necessary for the issue of a writ of quo-warranto are as follows:-

(a) The office must be public and it must be created by a statute or by the Constitution itself;

(b) The office must be a substantive one and not merely the function or employment of a servant at the will and during the pleasure of another; and

(c) There has been contravention of the Constitution or a statute or statutory instrument appointing such person to that office.

A public office will mean an office in which the public have an interest. In GD Karkare V TL Shebde; AIR 1962 Nagpur 330, the petitioner applied to the High Court for the issue of a writ of quo–warranto against the Advocate General of the State on the allegation that he was guilty of intrusion into the office of the Advocate General, for at the date of appointment he did not possess the necessary qualifications prescribed by the Constitution for that office. It was held that a writ of quo-warranto could be issued as the office of the Advocate General was of a public nature. An application for the writ of quo-warranto challenging the legality of an appointment to an office of a public nature is maintainable at the instance of any private person, although he is not personally aggrieved or interested in the matter.

Prohibition

A writ of prohibition commands the court or tribunal to whom it is issued to refrain from doing something which it about to do. It prevents a tribunal possessing judicial or quasi-judicial powers from assuming or threatening to assume jurisdiction which it does not possess. Thus, the writ lies both for excess of jurisdiction and absence of jurisdiction. Prohibition has much in common with certiorari, both in its scope and in the rules by which it is governed. Both these writs lie against a judicial or quasi-judicial body but not against an executive body. In Hari Vishnu Kamat V S Ahmad Ishaque; AIR 1965 SC 233, the Supreme Court said:

"Both the writs of prohibition and certiorari have for their object the restraining of inferior courts from exceeding their jurisdiction and they could be issued not merely to court, but to authorities exercising or quasi-judicial functions".

There is one fundamental distinction between the writs of prohibition and certiorari. They are issued at different stages of the proceedings. When an inferior court takes up for hearing a matter over which it has no jurisdiction, the person against whom the proceedings are taken can move to the superior court for a writ of prohibition, and on that, an order will be issued forbidding the inferior court from continuing the proceedings. On the other hand, if the court hears that case or matter and gives a decision, the party aggrieved will have to move the superior court for a writ of certiorari, and on that, an order will be made quashing the decision on the ground of want of jurisdiction.

The writ of prohibition differs from the writ of mandamus in that while the mandamus commands activity, prohibition commands inactivity. Further while mandamus is available not only against judicial authorities but also against administrative authorities, prohibition as also certiorari is issued only against judicial or quasi-judicial authorities.

Principles for exercise of jurisdiction. The following are some of the principles which would regulate the exercise of jurisdiction under Article 226:-

1. Alternative remedy
2. Delay
3. Suppersion of facts
4. Futile writ
5. Disputed question of fact
6. Perpetuation of illegulity
7. Dismissal in limine
8. Joinder of parties

Procedures

Procedure is a means towards the realization of justice. It is the machinery for achieving the goals embodied in the substantive law. Procedural law is often characterized as adjective law, as accessory to giving execution and effect to the substantive law. Procedural law do quite often play more important role than substantive law because it provides a mode, a path through which working in law courts have to be streamlined. The primary object of it is to complement, to breathe life into and give reality to the substantive law. The legislature often inserts, in the procedural Code itself savings regarding procedural irregularities. However there is a limit beyond which such provisions cannot operate. There is a clear difference between irregularities and illegalities. While an irregularity is curable, an illegality may result in a major infirmity which may become a disqualification.

Stages in Judicial Proceedings

Broadly put, the stages involved in a civil process or criminal matter are listed below.

I. **Civil Procedure Code**

1. Parties to suits.
2. Framing of suit.
3. Objection to jurisdiction.
4. Issue of summons.
5. Written Statements.
6. Appearance of parties, hearing of suit and examination of witnesses.
7. Settlement of issues.
8. Judgement.
9. Appeals.

II. **Criminal Procedure Code**

1. Information to the police and their powers to investigate.
2. Arrest.
3. Initiation of proceedings.
4. Complaints to Magistrates.
5. Framing of Charges.
6. Trial.
7. Judgement.
8. Appeal.

Civil Procedure Code

The Code of Civil Procedure (CPC), 1908 is one of the most important legislations. A number of its rules incorporate certain sound doctrines needed for the proper management of time and resources. CPC deals with jurisdiction of courts, place of suing, institution of suits, issue of summons, judgements and decree, execution, incidental proceedings, suits in particular cases, special proceedings, appeals, reference, review and revision. The body of CPC also contains various schedules and appendices. These state as to who shall be parties, how a suit is to be framed, pleadings, plaint, written statements, appearance of parties and their examination, admission, production, impounding and return of documents, settlement of issues, disposal, hearing of the suits, affidavits and matters like death, marriage and insolvency of parties.

Parties to Suit

In law, party is a synonym for litigant. A suit whether under Section 92 of the CPC or under Order 1 Rule 8 of CPC is to be filed by the representatives of a large number of persons who have a common interest. The very nature of a representative suit makes all those who have common interest in the suit as parties. Where it appears to the court that any joinder of plaintiffs may embarrass or delay the trial of the suit, the court may put the plaintiffs to their election or order separate trials or make such other order as may be expedient. "Party to the Suit" for the purpose of Section 7 (iv-A)(i) of the Court Fees Act 1970, includes minor plaintiff on whose behalf suit is filed. The word **Suit** has not been defined in the Code. It means a proceedings instituted in a civil court by the presentation of a plaint. But the plain and grammatical meaning of the word would include the whole of the suit and not a part of the suit. Suit is a proceeding which commences with a petition in the nature of a plaint and the claim should be one triable by a court.

Framing of a Suit

A pleader before the filing of the suit should decide how the suit is to be framed? What relief should be claimed and what causes of action should be mentioned in the suit. A relief that a party omits to claim without reasonable cause of action cannot be granted in a subsequent suit for same cause of action. Order 2 Rule 1 CPC provides that every suit is as far as practicable to be framed so as to afford ground for final decision upon the subjects in dispute and to prevent further litigation concerning them. The plaintiff must allege all titles in one and the same suit; in other words, he must raise all grounds of attack available to him with reference to his claim. Cause of action for the purpose of this Rules means all the essential facts constituting the right and its infringement. There is a builtin mechanism by which every debt, howsoever big or small, owing by the Government would be duly discharged. Any creditor of the Government can file a suit for recovery of a debt and, once a decree is obtained, the amount becomes automatically charged on the Consolidated Fund of India under Article 112 of the Constitution, and Article 113 provides that even Parliament has no right to vote upon it.

Issue and Service of Summons

When a suit has been duly instituted a summons may be issued to the defendant to appear and answer the claim on a day to be therein specified. A defendant to whom a summon has been so issued may appear

- in person, or
- by a pleader duly instructed and able to answer all material question.
- by a pleader accompanied by some person able to answer all such questions.

Every summon shall be signed by the judge or such officer as he appoints and shall be sealed with the seal of the court. Every summon shall be accompanied by a copy of the plaint, or if so permitted, by concise statement. Where the court sees reason to require personal appearance of the defendant, the summons shall order him to appear in person in court on the day therein specified (Order V Rule 1).

Where the defendant resides within the jurisdiction of the court in which the suit is instituted or has an agent resident within that jurisdiction who is empowered to accept the service of the summons, the summons shall, unless the court otherwise directs, be delivered or sent to the proper officer to be served by him or one of his subordinates. Service of the summons shall be made by delivering or tendering a copy thereof signed by the Judge or such officer as he appoints in this behalf, and sealed with the seal of the court. Where the serving officer delivers or tenders a copy of the summons to the defendant personally, or to an agent or other person on his behalf, he shall require the signature of the person to whom the copy is so delivered or tendered to an acknowledgement of service endorsed on the original summon (Section 79).

Written Statements

Pleading shall mean plaint or written statement. Pleadings are required to state material facts and not evidence. Order 6 deals with pleadings in general. Order 7 deals with plaints and Order with written statements. The fundamental rule of pleadings require four things :

(a) Every pleading must state facts and not law.

(b) It must state material facts and material facts only.

(c) It must state only the facts on which the party making the pleading relies for his claim or defence, and not the evidence by which they are to be proved.

(d) It must state such facts in a concise form.

The defendant shall, at or before the first hearing or within such time as the court may permit, present a written statement of his defence. The written statement is required to contain a statement, in a concise form of the material facts on which the party pleading relies for his defence. It is not to contain the evidence by which those facts are to be proved. A defendant may by his written statement raise as many distinct and separate, and therefore, inconsistent defences as he may think proper, provided the pleading is not embarrassing.

Appearance of Parties

Order IX deals with these aspects. Vide Section 86 on the day fixed in the summons for the defendant to appear and answer, the parties shall be in attendance at the court, whether in person or by their respective pleaders, and the suit shall then be heard unless the hearing is adjourned to a future day fixed by the court. Where neither party appears when the suit is called on for hearing, the court may make an order that the suit be dismissed. If the defendant does not appear, and it is proved that the summon was duly served upon him, the court may proceed ex-parte. If the plaintiff makes out a prima facie case, the court may pass a decree for the plaintiff.

Settlement of Issues

Order XIV pertains to settlement of issues and determination of suit on issue of law or on issues agreed upon. Issues arise when a material proposition of fact or law is affirmed by one party and denied by the other. Material propositions are those propositions of law or fact which a plaintiff must allege in order to show a right to sue or a defendant must allege in order to constitute his defence. Each material proposition affirmed by one party and denied by the other shall form the subject of a distinct issue. Issues are of two kinds viz., issues of fact or issues of law. At the first hearing of the suit, the court shall after reading the plaint and the written statements, if any, and after examination and after hearing the parties or their pleaders, ascertain upon what material propositions of fact or of law the parties are at variance, and shall thereupon proceed to frame and record the issues on which the right decision of the case appears to depend.

Judgement

The court is required to pronounce judgement on all issues. The court after the case has been heard, shall pronounce judgement in open court, either at once or as soon thereafter as may be practicable on some future day and when the judgement is to be pronounced on some future day, the court shall fix a day for the purpose of which due notice shall be given to the parties or their pleaders. Where a written judgement is to be pronounced, it shall be sufficient if the findings of the court on each issue and the final order passed in the case are read out. It shall not be necessary for the court to read out the whole judgement but a copy of the whole judgement shall be made available for perusal of the parties or the pleaders immediately after the judgement is pronounced. The judgement shall be dated and signed by the judge in open court at the time of pronouncing it and, when once signed, shall not afterwards be altered or added to. Order 20 CPC concerns the sections applicable in this regard.

Appeals

Order XLI CPC relates to appeals from original decrees. Every appeal is required to be preferred in the form of a memorandum. It is to be signed by the appellant or his pleader. It is to be presented to the court or to such officers as it appoints in this behalf. The memorandum is to be accompanied by a copy of the decree appealed from and of the judgement on which it is founded. The memorandum shall set forth concisely the grounds of objection to the decree appealed from. The grounds of objection must be such as arise from the pleadings and evidence, and are necessary for the decision of the case. Where an appeal is presented after the expiry of the period of limitation specified therefore, it shall be accompanied by an application supported by affidavit setting forth the facts on which the appellant relies to satisfy the court that he had sufficient cause for not preferring the appeal within such period.

"Laws not enforced cease to be laws, and rights not defended wither away."

-Thomas Moriarty

The Specific Relief Act, 1963

It is the duty of the State to see that no one encroaches upon the rights of another. Specific relief, as a form of judical redress, belongs to the Law of Procedure. "Specific Relief" is a particular relief to which a person is entiled in the first instance as distinguished from compensatory relief. Specific relief can be granted only for the purpose of enforcing individual civil rights and not for the mere purpose of enforcing a penal law.

A person entitled to the possession of specific immovable property may recover it in the manner provided by the Code of Civil Procedure, 1908 (Section 5). If any person is disposed without his consent of immovable property otherwise than in due course of law, he or any person claiming through him may, by suit, recover possession thereof, notwithstanding any other title that may be set up in such suit (Section 6).

A person entitled to the possession of specific movable property may recover it in the manner provided by the Code of Civil Procedure, 1908 (Section 7).Specific performance of the contract granted by the court to the aggrieved party is the specific relief which he may seek from the court and to which he is entitled. In à suit for specific performance of a contract, the defendant may plead any ground which is available to him under any law relating to contracts, such as incapacity of parties, absence of a concluded contract, coercion, fraud, misrepresentation, mistake, illegality, or want of authority to enter into the contract. Specific performance of a contract is a remedy by which a party to a contract is compelled to do or omit the very acts which he has undertaken to do or omit. Specific performance is an equitable relief and he who seeks equity must do equity to the opposite party.s

The specific performance of any contract may, in the discretion of the court, be enforced – (a) when there exists no standard for ascertaining the actual damaged caused by the non-performance of the act agreed to be done; or (b) when the act agreed to be done is such that compensation in money for its non-performance would not afford adequate relief (Section 10).

Kinds of Specific Relief

1. Specific Performance
   (a) Recovery of possession of property.
   (b) Specific performance of contract.
2. Injunction
   (a) Injunction generally.
   (b) Perpetual injunction.
3. Declaratory decrees
4. Rectification of instruments.
5. Recession of contracts.
6. Cancellation of instruments.

Declaratory Decree. It is a decree which declares that the plaintiff is entitled to any legal character or to any right as to any property against the defendant who denies his title to such character or right.

Kinds of Injunction

1. Temporary, interlocutory or ad-inter.
2. Perpetual or permanent.
3. Mandatory.
4. Ex-parte.

Injunction. Where a party is in breach of a negative term of a contract i.e. where he is doing something which he promised not to do; the court may by issuing an order restrain him from doing what he promised not to do. Such an order of the court is known as an injunction.

Contracts Not Specific Enforceable

The following contracts cannot be specifically enforced namely

(a) A Contract for non-performance of which compensation in money is an adequate relief.

(b) A Contract which runs into such minute or numerous details or which is so dependent on the personal qualifications or volition of the parties, or otherwise from its nature is such that the court cannot enforce specific performance of its material terms;

(c) A Contract which is in its nature determinable.

(d) A Contract the performance of which involves the performance of continuous duty which the court cannot supervise (Section 14)

Rescission of Contracts

Rescission refers to the undoing of a thing. Any person interested in a contract may sue to have it rescinded, and such rescission may be adjudged by the court in any of the following cases, namely :-

(a) where the Contract is voidable or terminable by the plaintiff.

(b) Where the Contract is unlawful for causes not apparent on its face and the defendant is more to blame than the plaintiff (Section 27).

Any person entitled to any legal character or to any right as to any property, may institute a suit against any person denying or interested to deny his title to such character or right and the court may in its discretion make therein a declaration that he is so entitled and the plaintiff need not in such suit ask for any further relief (Section 905). A perpetual injunction may be granted to the plaintiff to prevent the breach of an obligation existing in his favour, whether expressly or by implication (Section 38). A perpetual injunction means an injunction granted upon the final trial.

Criminal Procedure Code

The law relating to criminal procedure applicable to all criminal proceedings in India (except those in the States of Jammu & Kashmir and Nagaland and the tribal areas in Assam) is contained in the Code of Criminal Procedure, 1998. The Code has been amended from time to time by various acts of the Central and State Legislatures. The more important of these were the amendments brought about by Central legislation in 1923 and 1955. The amendments of 1955 were extensive and were intended to simplify procedures and speed up trials as far as possible. The object of the Code is to provide a machinery for the punishment of offences against the substantive criminal law and to ensure to the accused a fair trial for the ascertainment of his guilt or innocence.

Different chapters of the Cr PC lay down detailed provisions relating to the mode in which it is to be ascertained by whom an alleged offence has been committed and the mode in which he should be tried and punished by a competent court. Cr PC deals with matters like constitution of criminal courts and their power, arrest of persons, process to compel appearance and production of things, security for keeping peace and for good behaviour, grant of maintenance, maintenance of public order and tranquility, preventive action of the police, investigation, inquiries, trial proceedings, complaints to Magistrates and courts of session, evidence, accused persons of unsound mind, judgement, death sentence, appeal, reference and revision, transfer, execution of sentences, bail, disposal of property.

First Information Report

FIR is the first step in almost all cases of investigation and its importance lies as to know the facts at the earliest opportunity and it gives momentum to investigation. The condition which is *sine qua non* for recording a FIR is that there must be an information and that information must disclose a cognizable offence. The object of FIR from the point of view of the information is to set the criminal law in motion. It need not be made by an eye-witness nor it is required to give full details. It must not be vague or indefinite. It must be the earliest report relating to the commission of such offence made to a Police Officer. The information must relate to the commission of a cognizable offence. From the point of view of the investigating authorities it is to obtain information about the alleged criminal activity so as to be able to take suitable steps for tracing and bringing to book the guilty party. The FIR is not a substantive piece of evidence. It can be used for corroborating or contradicting its maker when he appears in person as a witness.

FIR is registered on the basis of the statements given by the victim or the witnesses and details are always incorporated immediately in that. An FIR is always an initiation of investigation and facts as they are revealed are brought on record on recured on the basis of stage by stage investigation.

Complaint

A complaint means any allegation made orally or in writing to a Magistrate, with a view to his taking, action under the Cr PC that some person whether known or unknown has committed an offence but it does not include a police report.

The receipt of a complaint is one of the modes according to which a Magistrate can take cognizance of an offence. The allegation must be of the fact that some person, whether known or unknown, has committed an offence. The complaint should be examined immediately after a Magistrate has taken cognizance of an offence on a complaint.

The object of the examination of the complainant and his witnesses who are present at the earliest stage is to ascertain whether there is a prima facie case against the person accused of the offence in the complaint; and to prevent the issue of the process on a complaint which is either false or vexatious or intended only to harass him. If the complaint is made to a Magistrate who is not competent to take cognizance of the offence, he shall if the complaint is in writing, return it for presentation to the proper court with an endorsement to the effect. On the other hand, if the complaint is not in writing, direct the complainant to proper court.

What is the difference between an FIR and a complaint?

The magistrate can take cognisance of an offence on a complaint, but not on first information. Any person can give the first information, but a complaint can be given only by a person authorised under the law under certain circumstances. It is only when a valid complaint is given that the court can take cognisance of it. First information on the other hand, only empowers the police officer to start investigation in cases of cognizable offence.

Investigations

Investigation is of prime importance in the trial of a case. Chapter XII of the Cr PC deals with the "Information to the Police and their Powers to Investigate".

It casts a duty on the officer-in-charge of a police station to reduce to writing every information relating to commission of cognizable offence given to him and the same will be read over to the informant and the same shall be signed by the informant and a copy thereof shall be given to him. The commencement of investigation in a cognizable offence by a police officer is subject to two conditions. Firstly, the police officer should have reason to suspect the commission of a cognizable offence as required under Cr PC Section 157(1) and secondly, the police officer should subjectively satisfy himself as to whether there is sufficient ground for entering on an investigation even before he starts an investigation in to the facts and circumstances of the case.

Investigation is the foundation on which the whole case rests and revolves. It consists of various steps viz.,

(a) Proceeding to the spot.

(b) Ascertainment of the facts and circumstances of the case.

(c) Discovery and arrest of the suspected offender.

(d) Collection of evidence relating to commission of the offence, which may consist of :-

   (i) The examination of various persons including the accused and the reduction of their statements into writing, if the officer thinks fit.

   (ii) The search of places of seizure of things considered

necessary for the investigation and to be produced at the trial.

(e) Formation of opinion as to whether on the material collected, there is a case to place the accused before a Magistrate for trial, and if so, taking the necessary steps for the same by filing of a charge sheet.

Search Warrant

A search warrant is a warrant issued by a court for the search of a place to be executed in the same way as a warrant for arrest of a person. Search is a more efficacious remedy than a mere summon to produce a document or thing and is accordingly a more drastic step. Issuing a search warrant is a judicial act which can be done only if there are sufficient materials on the record to induce the court to be prima facie satisfied. The search should be made in the presence of two or more respectable witnesses of the locality and list of the things seized in the course of such search and of places in which they are expected to be found shall be prepared by the searching officers and signed by the witnesses.

Arrest

Arrest is restraining of the liberty of a man's person in order to compel obedience to the order of a court of justice, or to prevent the commission of crime, or to ensure that a person charged or suspected of crime may be forthcoming to answer it. In ordinary and natural sense, arrest means apprehension or restraint on the deprivation of one's personal liberty. To constitute arrest there must be an intent to arrest under the authority accompanied by seizure or detention of the person in the manner known to law. Arrest may be effected under the following situations:-

(a) Under the civil law.

(i) Arrest of a judgement debtor in execution of a decree (Section 55 CPC); and

(ii) Arrest of a defendant before judgement under Order 38 of the CPC.

(b) Under the Criminal Law.

(i) Arrest by police without warrant and on suspicion of a cognizable offence (Section 41 Cr PC);

(ii) Arrest by a private person in a cognizable offence (Section 43 Cr PC;

(iii) Arrest by police in non-cognizable offence on refusal to give name and address (Section 42 Cr PC) ;

(iv) Arrest by Magistrate in case of commission of the offence in his presence (Section 44 Cr PC); and

(v) Arrest of escaped offender.

Section 46 Cr PC provides that in making an arrest the police officer or other person making an arrest "shall actually touch or confine the body of the person to be arrested, unless there be a submission to the custody by word or action". A person arrested has certain Fundamental Rights guaranteed by Article 22(1) and (2) of the Constitution read with Sections 50 and 57 Cr PC. Thus, he is to be informed of the grounds of arrest and of the right to bail in a non-bailable offence. Secondly, he cannot be detained for more than 24 hours without being produced before a Magistrate. Article 22(1) of the Constitution refers. He is entitled to have adequate time and facilities for preparation of his defence and to communicate with counsel of his choice. He cannot be compelled to testify against himself or to confess guilt.

Bail

Bail means the security taken from a person to appear on a fixed date before a court. It is the release of the accused from the custody of the officers of law and entrusting him to the private custody of persons who become bound as sureties to produce the accused to answer the charge at the stipulated time or date. It is a security for the appearance of the prisoner on giving which the accused is released pending trial. Person who is suspected to be involved in offence but who is neither arrested nor against whom any order for arrest is issued cannot be granted bail. The general policy of law is to allow bail rather than refuse it. It cannot be withheld as a measure of punishment.

The distinction between an ordinary order of bail and an order of anticipatory bail is that whereas the former is granted after arrest and therefore means release from the custody of the police, the later is granted in anticipation of arrest and is therefore effective at the moment of arrest. The over-riding considerations in granting bail shall be –

(a) Nature and gravity of circumstances in which offence is committed.

(b) The position and status of the accused with reference to the victim and the witnesses.

(c) Likelihood of the accused fleeing from justice, or of repeating the offence, or of jeopardizing his own life being faced with a grim prospect of possible conviction in the case.

(d) The likelihood of the accused tampering with the witnesses.

(e) History of the case as well as of its investigation and other relevant grounds which inview of many variable factors cannot be exhaustively set out. Court shall take into consideration whether the accused shall flee from justice or tamper with the prosecution evidence in the event of bail, as two paramount considerations.

Charge

A charge is an accusation made against a person in respect of an offence alleged to have been committed by him. The word 'charge' includes besides the element of offence, the reference to the person who is alleged to have committed it. It is an accusation made against a person in respect of an act committed or omitted in violation of a penal law forbidding or commanding it. It also mentions the particulars of the manner in which the alleged offence was committed besides a statement of the law and the section of the law against which the offence is said to have been committed.

A charge sheet is a paper kept at a police station to receive each night the names of the persons brought and taken into custody, the nature of the accusation and the name of the accuser in each case. It is under the custody of the inspector on duty. It is also called a 'challan' or police report. This report is made in the prescribed form. This also shows the names of the persons who appear to be acquainted with the circumstances of the case.

Trial

Trial means the examination and determination of a cause by a judicial tribunal or determination of guilt or innocence of an accused person by a court. The judicial functions of court begin as soon as the public prosecutor opens his case and has produced documents in support of his case. This begins after the accused is brought before the court. Hearing of arguments and consideration of documents produced by a party in the presence of the accused is the exercise of a judicial function and once that is done, the trial starts. A trial can conclude only in a conviction or acquittal.

In a warrant case, whether instituted on police report or otherwise, the 'trial commences only after framing of a charge against the accused, and in a summons case the 'trial' begins as soon as the accused appears before the court and the particulars of the offence are put to him.

Judgement

The word "judgement" means the expression of the opinion of the court arrived at after a due consideration of the evidence and all the arguments. Sections 353 to 365 of the Cr PC pertain to judgements. The criterion or basis for the criminal court to arrive at a conclusion relating to the guilt of the accused is in the admissible and relevant evidence oral and documentary adduced by the parties according to the provisions of the Evidence Act before it.

Appeal

A right of appeal is not a procedural but a substantive right. It is a vested right which can be taken away only by a subsequent enactment. The legal pursuit of a remedy continues from the date of commencement of a proceeding up to its disposal by a final court of appeal. An appeal is thus a continuation of the original proceeding. An appeal lies on grounds of law as well as fact. In a criminal appeal whether against a judgement of conviction or acquittal, it is for the prosecution to establish that the judgement of trial court is right or wrong.

Indian Evidence Act

In order to decide the right or liability of litigants there must be facts before the court. The parties to the proceeding and some times even courts prove facts which may form basis of decision. The time of the court is very precious. Bringing of irrelevant and frivolous facts on record wastes the time of the courts, prolongs the proceedings unnecessarily and also it may influence the mind of the court to the detriment of justice. Consequently, there should be some rule of law to control the leading of evidence in a judicial proceeding.

The Indian Evidence Act, 1872 is a Bible for every lawyer practicing in civil courts or criminal courts. It deals with matters like relevancy of facts, statement by persons who cannot be called as witnesses, statements made under special circumstance, opinion of third persons when relevant, character of accused persons or witnesses when relevant, facts which need not be proved, oral testimony, documentary evidence, public documents, presumption, burden of proof, estoppel, witnesses and their examination and lastly improper evidence & rejection of evidence.

There is no difference in principles between the method of enquiry in judicial and extra-judicial proceedings. In either case a person who wishes to find out whether a particular event did or did not happen tries, in the first place, to obtain information from persons who were present and saw what happened (direct evidence); failing that, he tries to obtain information from persons who can tell him about facts from which he can draw an inference as to whether the event did or did not happen (indirect evidence). But in judicial inquiries the information must be on oath or affirmation, and must be liable to be tested by cross-examination. The Indian Evidence Act (Section 5) by allowing evidence to be given only regarding facts which are "in issue" or "relevant" excludes particular classes of indirect evidence which an ordinary inquirer would naturally take into consideration. Statements so excluded are said to be "not admissible as evidence".

The law of evidence shows how a court may lawfully be convinced that the facts alleged in the charge happened or that their happening was so probable that it may be regarded as proved. The Indian Evidence Act deals with the subject thus–

(a) Part I and certain portions of Part III show what sort of facts may be proved in order to produce this conviction in the minds of the court.

(b) Part II deals with the proof of facts, that is, what sort of proof is to be given of those facts.

(c) The great portion of Part III deals with the procedure of that proof that is, who is to give it, and how it is to be given.

The definitions of 'proved', 'disproved' and 'not proved' as given in Section 3 are particularly noticeable. These are:-

'Proved'. "A fact is said to be proved, when after considering the matters before it, the court either believes it to exist or considers its existence so probable that a prudent man ought, under the circumstances of the particular case to act upon the supposition that it exists".

'Disproved'. A fact is said to be disproved when, after considering the matters before it, the court either believes that it does not exist or considers its non-existence so probable that a prudent man ought, under the circumstances of the particular case, to act upon the supposition that it does not exist".

'Not Proved'. A fact is said not to be proved when it is neither 'proved' nor 'disproved'.

Relevant facts

Chapter II of the IEA deals with "relevancy of facts". If a fact is not included in this enumeration of "relevant facts", it is inadmissible unless it is actually in issue, or its admission is specially provided for elsewhere under Sections 145, 146, 148, 153, 155, 157 and 158 IEA; or by some other provisions of law.

When can a conviction be based only on a dying declaration?

A truthful and reliable declaration may form the basis of conviction, even though it is not corroborated. The court should be satisfied that the declaration is truthful. The reliability should be subjected to close scrutiny, considering that it was made in the absence of the accused, who has had no opportunity to test its veracity, by means of cross examination. If a dying declaration is found to be reliable, voluntary and made by a person in a fit mental condition, corroboration is not necessary. Conviction for murder can be based solely on a dying declaration.

Public Interest Litigation

The subject of public interest litigation became very popular in the recent times. Public interest litigation is a unique phenomenon which visualizes the freedoms relating to Fundamental Rights interpreted humanistically in the light of Directive Principles of State Policy and making the court and instrument within the reach of dalits and other weaker sections. The three considerations which are emphasized in the matter of public litigation are :

(a) the person moving the court must have sufficient interest;

(b) there must be a public injury; or

(c) the action must be bonafide.

It is now established that a writ petition may be moved not only by an aggrieved individual but also by a public spirited individual or a journalist or a social action group, for the enforcement of the constitutional or legal rights of some other persons, provided such other person is unable to approach the court for redress. Even where no particular person has been legally injured but a public injury has been caused by the violation of a constitutional principle, such as the independence of judiciary, any person who is likely to be affected by such public injury, such as a lawyer, would be allowed to complain of such violation.

The court's approach should not be technical. There is no procedure prescribed for initiating a public interest litigation. Such motion may be made not only by a regular petition but also by a letter addressed to the court or even a telegram. Even if the petitioner withdraws from the proceedings, the proceedings can continue. The Supreme Court has held that "where a person or group of persons to whom injury caused by reason of violation of a fundamental right is unable to approach the court for judicial redress on account of poverty or disability or socially or economically disadvantaged position any member of the public acting bonafide can move the court for relief under Article 32 .... So that the fundamental rights may become meaningful not only for the rich and well-to-do who have the means to approach the court but also for the large masses of people who are undergoing a life of want and destitution and who are by reason of lack of awareness, assertiveness and resources are unable to seek judicial redress".

It would be interesting to take note of a few judgements in the sphere of public interest litigation that have a bearing on the industrial scene. It was held that Articles 21 and 23 of the Constitution require the identification and release of bonded labour and their rehabilitation too. (Neerja Choudhary V State of M.P.; AIR 1984 SC 1099). Right to healthy life is an obligation of the State both under Article 21 and Article 47 (State of Punjab V Ramlubhaya Bagga; (1998) 4 SCC 117. Where there was demolition of unauthorized construction and claim of compensation, it was held that there was no public interest involved and the same cannot be entertained as a PIL (Dalit Singh Dalal V State of M.P.; 1989(2) Scale 1012 where the Scheduled Tribes in possession of the property assigned to them were prosecuted for trespass etc, the Court had disposed of the writ petition directing the issuance of *patta* and also stay of the criminal cases.

In Paramananda Kataria V Union of India, AIR 1989 SC 2039, where an injured citizen was brought for treatment, it was held that medical aid is to be given to preserve life and thereafter the procedure of criminal law is to be followed. A number of significant directions were given with regard to the sick industries and workmen in the case of workers of M/s Rohtas Ltd V M/s Rohtas Industries Ltd; 1989(2) Scale 873. The aspect of child labour and compensation to the victims of accident were carefully analysed by the Supreme Court in MC Mehta V State of Tamil Nadu; 1991(2) Scale 464.

The directions given by the Supreme Court in Buffalow Trades Welfare Association V Ms Maneka Gandhi, 1996(11) SCC 35 may be relevant in any future situation involving food processing industry. So would be the policy enunciated in the Akhila Bharat Go Sewa Sangh V State of A.P; 1994(4) Scale 721. The upper limit with regard to capacity of plant and affluents in the case of tanneries was examined by the Supreme Court in M/s Jayman Tanners Association case; AIR 2000 SC 150. On the other hand, there are numerous cases where the courts declined to view the matter as involving public interest. Where allegations of omission and commission on the part of public center undertakings were alleged, the court held that PIL should not be allowed to act as a vehicle of harassment. It being *pro bono* public should not smack of any ulterior motive as no person can be permitted to achieve any personal gain or ulterior purposes thereby. (Milan Kumar Pradhan V Union of India, AIR 2000 Calcutta 5). In a PIL public interest must be real and it must not be to invoke further cause of enmity. (Delhi Municipal Workers Union (Regd) V Delhi Municipal Corporation; AIR 2001 Delhi 68)

Judicial Precedents

Judicial precedents are an important source of law based on the principle that what has been decided in an earlier case is binding in a similar future case unless there is a change in the circumstances. This is called doctrine of precedents which means adherence to the earlier decision and not unsettling thing which are already established.

Judgements delivered by the superior courts are regarded as much a part of the law of the country as legislative enactments. The practice of following precedents is necessary to secure the certainty of law and predictability of decisions. Further this creates confidence in the minds of litigants and the administration of justice becomes fair.

Supreme Court decisions are binding on all Courts within the territory of India (Article 141 of the Constitution of India). If on a subsequent occasion the Court is satisfied that its earlier decision was clearly erroneous, it may "correct the error", but before a previous decision pronounced to be plainly erroneous, the Court must be satisfied with a fair amount of unanimity amongst its members that revision of the said view is fully justified. Further, the decisions of the Full Bench are binding on the smaller Benches of the Court.

The decisions of a High Court are binding on all the Courts below it, within its jurisdiction. The decisions of one High Court are not binding on the other High Courts, although in practice they are cited in other High Courts. These decisions, therefore, have only a persuasive value, but quite often, High Courts follow the rulings of each other on the ground of judicial uniformity, specially in the case of Central Acts. The decisions of a larger bench are binding on a smaller bench.

A court may disregard a precedent either by : (1) overruling it, or (2) refusing to follow it or dissenting from it. A precedent can be overruled by a Court of superior jurisdiction. When a Court 'dissents' from a precedent, it lays down new rules of law. When two Courts of co-ordinate jurisdiction differ with each other, the conflict can be resolved only by a superior court. Till this is done, the law remains uncertain.

7

Alternative Disputes Redressal

"Fools and obstinate men make lawyers rich"

Thomas Fuller

Arbitration

Arbitration involves the determination of a matter indispute by the judgement of one or more persons, called arbitrators, who in case, of differences usually call in an 'umpire' to decide between them.

An arbitration is the reference of a dispute or difference between not less than two parties for determination, after hearing both sides in a judicial manner, by a person or persons other than a court of competent jurisdiction. The essence of arbitration is that some dispute is referred by the parties for settlement to a tribunal of their own choosing instead of a court. In popular parlance, arbitration may be defined as a private process set up by the parties as a substitute for court litigation to obtain a decision on their disputes. Arbitration may be :

(a) Domestic arbitration.

(b) International arbitration.

(c) Ad-hoc arbitration.

(d) Institutional arbitration.

(e) Specialised arbitration; and

(f) Statutory arbitration.

The process of arbitration is governed by the Arbitration and Conciliation Act, 1996. It provides a unified regime for both international commercial arbitration and domestic arbitration of all types and also for conciliation. The salient features of the process as envisaged under the Act are that there has to be a written arbitration agreement. This may take the form of an arbitration clause in a contract or in a separate agreement. The process of arbitration may continue even when the dispute is pending before a judicial forum as subject of an arbitration agreement. The parties are free to determine number of arbitrators failing which arbitral tribunal shall consist of a sole arbitrator. An arbitrator may be challenged on grounds laid down e.g. doubts about his independence or impartiality etc.

Essentials of an Arbitration Agreement

1. It must be in writing.
2. It must have all the essential elements of a valid contract.
3. It must refer a dispute, present or future, between the parties.
4. It may be in the form of an arbitration clause or in the form of a separate agreement.

The place of arbitration is to be decided by the parties. The process should ensure equal treatment of parties. The proceedings are required to commence on the date on which request for dispute to be referred for arbitration is received by the respondent. The parties are free to determine language of the proceedings. Statement of claim and defence is to be made within the period of time agreed by the parties or determined by the arbitrator. While making a statement or claim, the facts supporting it are to be stated. The points in issue are to be identified. The relief or remedy sought is to be stated. All relevant documents are to be submitted. The claim and reply once filled may be amended or supplemented subsequently. The time-table and modalities of hearing and written proceedings are determined by him. He may appoint one or more experts to examine specific issued and report to him.

The tribunal is expected to decide the matter in accordance with the terms of contract and usages of trade applicable to the transaction. In situations involving more than one arbitrators, the decision is to be taken by majority of members. They are expected to encourage settlement by mediation and conciliation etc. The arbitral award must be in writing. It is required to give reasons for its award. If a recourse is sought against arbitral award, then an application is to be filed to a court for its setting aside. The grounds for revocation of authority of an arbitrator are as under:-

(a) Excess or refusal of jurisdiction by the arbitrator.

(b) Misconduct of arbitrator.

(c) Disqualification of arbitrator.

(d) Charges of fraud.

(e) Exception cases.

The grounds for setting aside an arbitral award are as under:-

(a) Incapacity of party.

(b) Agreement not valid under the law.

(c) Want of proper notice or unable to present his case.

(d) Matters beyond scope.

(e) Improper composition of the tribunal.

(f) Subject matter incapable of settlement.

(g) Award in conflict with public policy.

On finality, the arbitral award is to be enforced as if it was a decree of the court. An appeal against orders of arbitral council can be entertained on specified grounds only.

An arbitrator is duty bound to be fair and impartial without any bias. He is to observe principles of natural justice. This involves the doctrine that no one can be a judge in his own case. A duty is cast to act honestly and impartially. Reasonable and sufficient opportunity is to be provided to the parties. He is not to misconduct himself or the proceedings. He is forbidden to accept any gratification or pecuniary inducement. He is expected to give sufficient opportunity to the parties to present their case. He is empowered to proceed ex-parte if a party does not appear after due notice.

Advantages of Arbitration

1. Avoidance of publicity.
2. Simplicity of procedure.

3. Avoidance of delay and uncertainty involved in appeals.
4. Reduction of expenses.
5. Less time consuming.
6. Decision by a technical expert.
7. Social efficacy.
8. Candour in presenting facts and figures.

The two main disadvantages are based on incompetence or biased arbitrator and informality of the procedure.

Negotiation

It is a non-binding procedure involving direct interaction of the disputing parties, wherein a party approaches the other with the offer of negotiated settlement based on an object assessment of each other's position.

Mediation and Conciliation

Conciliation is a non-binding procedure in which an impartial third party, the conciliator, assists the parties to a dispute in reaching a mutually agreed settlement of the dispute. Mediation and conciliation are interchangeable expressions. In mediation the parties have the freedom to agree as they please and the mediator decides nothing, advises as to nothing. He helps parties agree, without himself/herself reaching or announcing a conclusion or decision. He shall be guided by the principles of objectivity, fairness and justice.

The conciliator is not bound by the Code of Civil Procedure or the Indian Evidence Act.

The conciliator may conduct the proceedings in such a manner as he considers appropriate taking into account–

(a) The circumstances of the case.

(b) The wishes the parties may express, including any request by a party that the conciliator hear oral statements; and

(c) The need for a speedy settlement of the dispute.

8

Human Rights and National Human Rights Commission

"It may be true that the law cannot make a man love me. But it can keep him from lynching me; and I think that's pretty important."

Martin Luther King, Junior

The United States defined human rights in a policy document in 1978 and said:

"Freedom from arbitrary arrest and imprisonment; tortures; unfair trial; cruel and unusual punishment; and invasion of privacy. Rights to food, shelter, health care and education and freedom of thought, speech, assembly, religion, press, movement and participation in Government."

Human rights may be described as those rights which belong to all human beings – regardless of their religion, colour, caste, race, sex, language, political beliefs or national origin – which allow them to preserve their dignity and to secure the healthy development of their personalities, and which enable them to live in peace and harmony with their fellow beings. Human rights are often described as "inalienable and imprescriptible". "Inalienable" means that these rights cannot be bartered or traded away. The term "imprescriptible" means that these rights cannot be taken away or withdrawn. They belong to every person as long as he or she is alive.

In India, the protection of Human Rights Act, 1993 defined human rights as 'The Rights relating to liberty' equality and dignity of the individual guaranteed by the Constitution of India as embodied in the fundamental rights and international covenants.

The scope of the human rights concept is expanding day by day. Broadly they fall into categories of:

(a) **Civil and political rights**. These include :

(i) Right to equality and non-discrimination.

(ii) Right to life and liberty.

(iii) Right against arbitrary arrest.

(iv) Right against self-incrimination.

(v) Freedom of movement.

(vi) Freedom of thought and expression.

(vii) Right to assemble peacefully.

(viii) Right to property.

(ix) Freedom of conscience and religion.

(x) Right against slavery.

(xi) Right to privacy.

(xii) Right to nationality.

(xiii) Equal access to public services.

(xiv) Right to take part in public affairs.

(xv) Right to from association.

(xvi) Cultural rights.

(b) **Economic, social and cultural rights**. These include

(i) Right to work.

(ii) Right to social security.

(iii) Right to equal pay for equal work.

(iv) Right to leisure.

(v) Right to protection of motherhood and childhood.

(vi) Right to education.

(vii) Right to protection of moral and material interest.

(viii) Right to strike.

(ix) Right to trade unions.

(x) Right to marriage and family.

(xi) Right to maternity benefits.

(xii) Right to minimum standard of living.

(xiii) Right to cultural life.

(c) **Group rights**. These include right of minorities and following :-

(i) The Rights of Women.

(ii) The Rights of Child.

(iii) The Rights of Indigenous People.

(iv) The Rights of Disabled.

(v) The Rights of Prisoners.

The Indian judiciary, especially at High court and Supreme Court levels, has been very supportive of human rights. Despite suffering constant resource constraints and the increasing pressures of case overload, the courts have tirelessly exerted themselves in the cause of protecting the individuals from being treated oppressively either by the State or by private entities.

National Human Rights Commission

National Human Rights Commission has been set up under the Protection of Human Rights Act. 1993, NHRC consists of:

(a) A Chairperson, who has been Chief Justice of India;

(b) One Member who is, or has been a Judge of Supreme Court.

(c) One Member who is, or has been, the Chief Justice of High Court

(d) Two Members to be appointed from amongst persons having knowledge of, or practical experience in matters relating to human rights.

National Human Rights Commission has been entrusted with following functions, namely :-

(a) It can inquire *suo motu* or on receiving a complaint of violation of human rights or abatement thereof, and negligence in prevention of such violation by a public servant.

(b) It can intervene in any proceeding involving any allegation of violation of human rights pending before a court, with the approval of such Court.

(c) It can visit any jail or any other institution where the persons are detained to study the living conditions of inmates.

(d) It can review the factor, including the act of terrorism that inhibits the enjoyment of human rights.

The Commission while inquiring into complaints shall have all the powers of a civil court trying a suit under the Civil Procedure Code, 1908. It can summon and enforce the attendance of witnesses and examine them on oath. Commission can also order for production of document before it and can receive evidence on affidavit. Every proceeding before the Commission shall be deemed to be a judicial proceeding within the mean of Section 193 and 228, and for purpose of Section 196 of Indian Penal Code and the Commission shall be deemed to be a civil court for the purpose of Section 198 and Chapter XXVI of the Code of Criminal Procedure Code, 1973.

The Commission while inquiring into the complaints of violation of human rights may call for any information or report from the Central Govt or any State Govt or any other authority or organization, within such time as may be specified by it. Where the inquiry discloses the violation of human rights, or negligence in prevention of such violation by a public servant, it may recommend the Central Govt. or the other authorities for initiation of proceeding for prosecution or for any other action as the Commission deems fit. Commission can approach Supreme Court and High Courts for such directions, orders or writs as the Court may deem necessary. It may recommend the concerned Govt. or the authority for the grant of such immediate interim relief to the victim or the member of his family as it considers necessary.

Illustrations may be given of different situation when the courts have applied human rights considerations in matters concerning corporate affairs.

(a) Essential Commodities. The requirement of a licence from traders engaged in the business of essential commodities is valid as a reasonable restriction as it is through licensing that the objects of Essential Supplies Act could be achieved.

(b) Imports and Exports. From time to time the Government issues policy statements and it has the right to change, revise or alter the policy as and when it desires to do so. It also canalises imports and exports of certain commodities through specialized channels, and in those commodities the Government has power to refuse to issue export or import licences to individuals or firms. This was held reasonable in Daya V Joint Controller Imports & Exports; AIR 1962 SC 1796

(C) Sugar Mills. In Lord Krishna Sugar Mills V UOI; the matter concerned an obligation imposed by law on sugar mills to hand over a certain percentage of their production to a Government agency for export. This was intended with a view to earn foreign exchange. The export price realized was less than the price fixed for sugar for internal consumption. The law was held valid.

(d) Metal Industry. In Indian Metal V Industrial Tribunal; AIR 1953 Mad 88; a factory was closed by giving 14 days notice to the employees. Upholding the closure, the court held that, "If a citizen has got a right to carry on business we think it follows that, he must be at liberty not to carry on if he so chooses. A person can no more be compelled to carry on a business than a person can be compelled to acquire or hold property".

(e) Mica Trade. In Mineral Development CorporationLtd. V State of Bihar; AIR 1960 SC 468; the power to cancel a licence was held valid since this could be exercised only on specified reason and the licencee was provided with an opportunity of being heard.

(f) Pharmaceutical. In Hindustan Antibiotic V Workmen; AIR 1967 SC 948, the Supreme Court held that there was a socio-economic justification for providing minimum wages to the worker because it is necessary for their social and economic upliftment.

Environmental Law

The environment consists of all, or any of the following media, namely the air, water and land and the medium of air includes the air within buildings and the air within other natural or man made structures above or below ground.

Environmental degradation is closely related to the pattern of resource-use permitted within society. Government is conscious about the fact that the presence of pollutants discharged through industrial emission etc. beyond certain limits disturbs the ecological balance and adversely affect public health as also the vegetation, property and monuments.

The Right to Breath and Right to Drink are two important underlying objectives in this regard.

Articles 47, 48A and 51A(g) of the Constitution of India specifically deal with environment. Indian Penal Code Section 277 provides for penalty for water pollution whereas Section 278 deals with air pollution. Sections 268, 269, 291, 426, 430, 431 and 432 relate to general pollution and their respective punishments. The powers of District and Sub-Division Magistrate to control various types of pollution are enumerated in Section 133, 143 and 144 of the Criminal Procedure Code. Regulation of music can be governed under Section 30 of the Police Act, 1861 whereas Section 34 prevents and controls slaughtering of animals, cleaning of carcass, cruelty to animals and throwing dirt into streets. Creative use can be made of Code of Civil Procedure and the Specific Relief Act, 1963 Section 34 to ensure protection of these natural rights.

A number of other legislations in the field of environment protection have been listed in Chapter 10. A few cases will illustrate jurisprudence of pollution.

In Gothan Construction Corporation V A.K. Ghosh; AIR 1968 Cal 91, running of a workshop in a residential colony was considered to be an act of causing nuisance and injury to the health of the citizens. In Gobind Singh V Shanti Swarup; AIR 1979 SC 143; the court dealt with situation involving pollution of air with smoke from a bakery causing injury as smoke emitted from its chimney in such a manner that it was injurious to health, safety and convenience of the people living in the close proximity of the bakery. In the case of Ratlam Municipality V Virdhi Chand; AIR 1980 SC 1622, the court handled the matter concerning failure of a municipality to prevent the discharge from an alcohol plant of malodorous fluids into the public streets.

The cases of Tarsem Singh V Mukund Singh Mistri; (1981 CC cases 232) and Ram Lal V Bari Singh; (1982 CC cases 189); related to air pollution caused by wheat thrasher and cotton grinding. Their operation producing day and night offensive suffocating dust storms was reported to have resulted in serious cough and skin diseases. In the case of Society for Protection of Silent Valley V Union of India, a petition was filed seeking a writ forbidding the State of Kerala from proceeding to construct a hydro electricity project at Silent Valley on the ground that it would adversely affect the Silent Valley and its environment. In Oleum Gas Leakage case; (1986) 2 SCC 176, the court confirmed the payment of compensation to the victims of Oleum gas. Right to healthy environment and its protection and the right to development are group rights and are loosely described as 'third generation rights.'

Gender Justice

Women forgive injuries, but never forget slights.

Haliburton

Articles 13, 14, 15 and 16 of the Constitution of India and other related articles prohibit discrimination on the ground of sex. Social and economic democracy is the cornerstone for success of political democracy. It is necessary to separate precepts from civil law. In matters of civil rights, laws of property and inheritance and marriage and divorce although practices may differ, legal rights that accrue must be the same. The Scheduled Castes, Scheduled Tribes and women have not infrequently suffered discrimination and social inequalities. It is mandatory, therefore, to render them socio-economic justice so as to ensure their dignity of person to bring them into the mainstream of the national life. The public policy and constitutional philosophy envisaged under Articles 14, 15(1) & (3) 38, 39 and 46 is to accord social and economic democracy to women as assured in the Preamble to the Constitution. They constitute the core foundation for economic empowerment and social justice to women. In other words, they frown upon gender discrimination and aim at elimination of obstacles to enjoy social, economic, political and cultural rights on equal footing.

Incidents of sexual harassment of women at workplace are indicative of fundamental rights violation of 'Gender Equality' and the 'Right to Life and Liberty' as enshrined under Articles 14, 15 and 21 of the Constitution. One of the logical consequences of such incidents is also the violation of the victim's fundamental right under Article 19(1)(g). The meaning and content of the fundamental rights guaranteed in the Constitution of India are of sufficient amplitude to encompass all the facets of gender equality including prevention of sexual harassment or abuse.

Such violations attract the remedy under Article 32 for the enforcement of these fundamental rights of women. A writ of mandamus in such a situation, to be actually effective, should be accompanied by directions for preventive measures. When instances of sexual harassment resulting in violation of fundamental rights of women workers under Articles 14, 19 and 21 are brought before for redress under Article 32, an effective redressal requires that some guidelines should be laid down for the protection of these rights to fill the legislative vacuum. By virtue of Article 73, the executive power of the Union is available till Parliament enacts legislation to expressly provide measures needed to curb the evil. Vishaka V State of Rajasthan, (1997) 6 SCC 241: 1997 SCC (Cri) 932; AIR 1997 SC 3011.

Harassment of Women at Workplaces; Prevention of:

Women at work place often become victims of sexual harassment cases. The Supreme Court of India has passed a landmark judgement for enforcement of human right of 'gender equality' and to prevent sexual harassment of women at workplaces. In the aforesaid case of Vishaka and Others V State of Rajasthan, the Supreme Court dealt with an alleged incident of brutal gang rape of a social worker in a village of

Rajasthan. The incident revealed the hazards to which a working woman may be exposed at her place of work, the lack of suitable mechanism for safeguarding them from sexual harassment as also a climate where the incidents of human rights violations are common.

In the absence of enacted laws to provide for effective enforcement of basic human right of gender equality and guarantee against sexual harassment and abuse, the Supreme Court laid down certain norms and guidelines as under :-

(a) It is the duty of employer or other responsible persons in work places and other institutions to prevent or deter the commission of acts of sexual harassment and to provide the procedure for resolution, settlement or prosecution of acts of sexual harassment by taking all steps required.

(b) For this purpose, sexual harassment includes such unwelcome sexually determined behaviour (whether directly or by implication) as:-

(i) physical contact and advances;

(ii) a demand or request for sexual favours;

(iii) sexually coloured remarks;

(iv) showing pornography;

(v) any other unwelcome physical, verbal or non-verbal conduct of sexual nature.

Any of the acts as indicated above would mean a humiliating conduct to attract adverse consequences.

(c) All employers or persons in charge of workplace should take appropriate steps to prevent sexual harassment at workplaces. Due publicity should be given and rules/ regulations of conduct made on the subject should include appropriate penalties.

(d) Where such conduct amounts to be specific offence under the IPC or under any other law, the employer shall initiate appropriate action in accordance with law by making a complaint with the appropriate authority. Victims of the sexual harassment should have the option to seek transfer of the perpetrator or their own transfer.

(e) Where such conduct amounts to misconduct in employment, appropriate disciplinary action should be initiated by the employer, as per the rules.

(f) Time-bound mechanism to deal with such complaints should be devised by the employer. Where necessary, a complaint committee, headed by a woman (and not less than half of its members should be women), and involving either an NGO or third party familiar with the issue of sexual harassment, should be formed. The Committee is required to submit its report to the Government Department.

(g) Where sexual harassment occurs as a result of an act or omission by a third party or the outsider, the employer and person in charge will take all necessary steps and should reasonably assist the affected person in terms of support and preventive action.

The Central and State Governments have been requested to adopt suitable measures including legislation to give effect to these guidelines in the Government as well as in the public and the private sectors. Even though the guidelines are quite elaborate, there are a few significant lacunae viz. non-provision of punishment to the accused or penalties to the employer; procedure of enquiry not made clear leading to criticism and isolation of the victim by other lady workers. Therefore, there is urgency to enact legislation to preserve, protect and promote the right of 'gender equality' and right to safety and dignity. The State should take steps to promptly enact suitable legislation to fill the vacuum and lacunae in the existing guidelines.

Child Labour

There are no illegitimate children—only illegitimate parents.

Leon R Yankwicho

Article 24 of the Constitution of India lays down, "No child below the age of fourteen years shall be employed to work in any factory or mine or engage in any other hazardous employment."

This Article is in line with clauses (e) and (f) of 39 clause (e) and (f) stipulates that :

(e) that the health and strength of workers, men and women, and the tender age of children are not abused and that citizens are not forced by economic necessity to enter avocations unsuited to their age or strength.

(f) That children are given opportunities and facilities to develop in a healthy manner and in conditions of freedom and dignity and that childhood and youth are protected against exploitation and against moral and material abandonment.

Article 45 lays down that the State shall endeavour to provide within the period of 10 years from the commencement of the Constitution, free and compulsory education for all children until they complete the age of 14 years. The Child Labour (Prohibition and Regulation) Act, 1986 presents a comprehensive legislation on child labour.

Note

9

The Law Lexicon

"Most of the disputes in the world arise from words".

William Murray, Ist Earl of Mansfield

Actionable Claim. This means-

(a) any unsecured debt.

(b) any interest in moveable property, not in possession of the claimant.

Ad-valorem. A term used in reference to the duties or custom paid on certain goods that is according to their value.

Affidavit. A written statement shorn before a person having authority to administer an oath, by a person called a deponent.

Affirmation. A solemn declaration without oath.

Amalgamation. This takes place where two incorporated Companies or Societies become united by one of them being merged in the other.

Assign. To transfer property, especially personal estate, or asset over a right to another.

Bail. To set at liberty a person arrested or imprisoned, on security being taken for his appearance on a day and at a place certain.

Bargain Price. It means a price that is stated in any advertisement to be a bargain price, by reference to an ordinary price or otherwise. It may also mean price that a person who reads, hears or sees the advertisement, would reasonably understand to be a bargain price having regard to the price at which the product advertised or like produce are ordinarily sold.

Bill of Credit. A licence or authority given in writing from one person to another, empowering a person to receive or take up money of their correspondents abroad.

Bonafide. Imply the absence of all fraud or unfair dealing.

Breach of Trust. A violation of duty by a trustee, executor or other person in a fiduciary position.

Burden of Proof. It is used in two distinct meanings in the Indian Evidence Act, viz the burden of establishing a case and the burden of introducing evidence. In a criminal trial, the burden of proving everything essential to the establishment of the charge against the accused lies upon the prosecution, and that burden never changes.

Bye Laws. Includes all orders, ordinances, regulations, rules and statutes made by any authority subordinate to the legislature. The subordinate authority must, of course, have power expressly or impliedly conferred on it to legislate on the matter to which the bye law relates.

Cause of Action. The expression comprises every fact which it would be necessary for plaintiff to prove if traversed, in order to support his right to the judgement of the court.

Caveat. A warning or caution. It is entered to stay the probate of a Will, letters of administration, a licence of marriage etc.

Cess. A cess is a tax levied for a specific purpose often with a prefixed word defining the object.

Citation. A reference to authorities in support of an argument.

Civil Courts. The Court consolidated for deciding purely civil question between persons seeking their civil rights and whose procedure is, in essence, governed by the Code of Civil procedure.

Clearing House. An institution organized by the banks of a city – the house through which bankers pass the bills and cheques they hold on other banks by a mutual arrangement. This is a place where bankers meet daily, adjust balances of accounts and receive and pay difference.

Cognizance. Judicial notice or knowledge. It takes place at a point when a Magistrate first takes judicial notice of an offence.

Collateral. The word is of frequent use in law where, it bears its ordinary significance of 'parallel' or 'additional'.

Consumer Dispute. This means a dispute where the person against whom a complaint has been made, denies or disputes the allegations contained in the complaint.

Contract. An enforceable covenant or agreement between two or more persons with a lawful consideration or cause.

Conveyance. An instrument which transfers property from one person to another.

Covenant. An agreement by deed between two or more persons to do one or more thing or things, or to give, or to prevent, or to refrain from something; an agreement creating an obligation.

Cross Examination. The examination of a witness by the party opposed to the party who has first examined him, in order to test the truth of such first or direction examination.

Dabba Trading. If refers to illegal or parralel stock market deals, those that aren't routed through the official exchanges.

Debt. if includes any liability in respect of any obligation to repay capital sums by way of annuties and any liability under any guarantee, and 'debt charges' shall be constructed accordingly.

Decree. The formal expression of an adjudication which, so far as regards the Court expressing it, conclusively determines the rights of the parties with regard to all or any of the matters in controversy in the suit and may be either preliminary or final.

Deed. A written or printed document between the parties purporting to effect some legal disposition.

Demurrage. An allowance or compensation for the delay or detention of vessel.

Deponent. A person who makes an affidavit or deposition.

Discharge. To free from liability, the act of freeing from obligation, the act of clearing off a pecuniary liability.

Disclaimer. A formal renunciation or the refusal to accept.

Dissolution. In general a break up; destroying; the relaxation of any tie or bond.

Earnest. Given as a token, the pledge dignifies a security by which we are engaged to indemnify for a loss.

Easement. A service or convenience or a right which the owner or occupier of a certain property possesses as such for the beneficial enjoyment of that property.

Endorsement. The signing of one's name on the back of a bill or note is an act which transfers the right in it to the endorse.

Endowment. It is dedication of property for purposes of religion or charity having both the subject and object certain and capable of ascertainment.

Equity, Justice. Equity is the moral redressing of what is legal, where owing to the imperfection of human laws, what is legal is not exactly just.

Estoppel. It is an admission or some thing which the law treats as an equivalent to an admission of so high and conclusive nature that any one who is affected by it is not permitted to contradict it.

Per Capita. Where distribution is to be per capita, the members of the class take the property to be distributed in equal shares, the individual alone being considered in the distribution.

Fee. Fee is a charge for special service rendered to individuals by some government agency.

FOB. An abbreviation for the words "free on board". The term denotes that the seller is to put the goods on board at his own expenses, but on account of, and thence forward at the risk and as property of, the purchaser.

Foreclose. To debar a mortgager from his right to redeem a mortgage.

Franchise. Privilege or exemption by privilege or grant.

Gift. Transfer of certain existing moveable or immoveable property made voluntarily and without consideration.

Good Faith. According to the Indian Penal Code, nothing is said to be done or believed in good faith which is done or believed without due care.

Goods. Every kind of movable property other than actionable claims and money; and includes stocks and shares.

Guarantee. It is a collateral engagement to answer for the debt, default or miscarriage of another person.

Hire. To acquire the temporary use of a thing or the services of a person in exchange for payment.

Holder. One who holds, a tenant, occupier, possessor or owner, the payee or endorsee of the bill or note, who is in possession of it, or the bearer thereof.

Hypothecation. A right which a creditor has over a thing belonging to another, and which consists in the power to cause it to be sold in order to be paid his claim out of the proceeds.

Incorporated Company. A corporation formed for the purpose of carrying on a business for profit.

Indemnity. To make good a loss which one person has suffered in consequence of the act or default of another.

Injunction. Authoritative order or judicial process restraining a person from wrongful act.

In Limine. At the outset, preliminary.

Insider Trading. Illegal insider trading relates to transactions conducted while in possession of material non-public information about the company or the script.

Laches. It is a neglect to do something which by law a man is obliged to do.

Lease. It is a conveyance by the owner of an estate to another of a portion of his interest for a term less than his own, in consideration of a certain annual or stated or other recompense.

Letter Patent. are a means whereby the crown makes a grant to a subject of some dignity, office, monopoly, franchise etc.

Licence. An authority to do something which would otherwise be in-operative, wrongful or illegal.

Lien. A charge on property for the payment of a debt or duty, and for which it may be sold in discharge of the lien. It signifies an obligation.

Limitation. It means the time which is prescribed by the authority of law, during which a title may be acquired to property by virtue of a simple adverse possession and enjoyment, of the time at the end of which no action or suit can be maintained.

Liquidated Damages. A sum stated and agreed to be paid as damages between the parties to a contract, in the event of default by either; the primary meaning of that phrase is, that the sum has been "assessed between the parties".

Merger. Is the destruction or "drowning" by operation of law of the less in the greater of two estates coming together and vesting without any intervening estate in one and the same person in the same right. "Whenever a greater estate and a less coincide and meet in one and the same person without any intermediate estate, the less is immediately annihilated, or in the law phrase is said to be merged that is, sunk or drowned in the great. Is the absorption or extinguishment of law not depending upon the intention of the parties." 'Merger' pre-supposes the existence of two independent things or estates, the greater of which would swallow up or may extinct the lesser one by the process of absorption.

Mortgage. The transfer of an interest in specific immoveable property for the purpose of securing the payment of money advanced or to be advanced by way of loan, an existing or future debt, on the performance of an engagement which may give rise to pecuniary liability. A mortgage is the conveyance of an estate by way of pledge for the security of a debt.

Negotiable Instrument. A 'negotiable instrument' means promissory note, bills of exchange or cheque payable either to order or to bearer.

Notification. It means a notification in the Official Gazette.

Not Negotiable. When a cheque or bill has these words written across its face they do not limit the transfer of it from one to another, but in the case of a transferor not having a good title to the document, the transfer is merely in the same position as the transferor, and cannot go back upon the original drawer for satisfaction.

Null. Of no legal force or effect; void; of no binding force or validity, of no efficacy; invalid; nugatory; useless.

Obiter Dictum. An opinion of law not necessary to the decision. An obiter dictum is an observation which is either not necessary for the decision of the case or does not relate to the material facts in issue.

Open Cheque. An uncrossed cheque payable on presentation to 'bearer' or 'order' as the case may be.

Patent. A grant from sovereign power securing to the inventor for a limited time the exclusive right to make use and vend the invention. It protects the first producer or inventor of an article against the manufacture, production and sale of any such article without his consent.

Payee. The person to whom a sum of money is to be paid; the person in whose favour a negotiable instrument has been drawn.

Pledge. A pledge is a transfer of personal property as a security for a debt or other obligation. The world 'pledge' is also used to describe the article or articles of personal property thus delivered by one person to another as security for the debt or obligation.

Power of Attorney. A formal instrument by which one person empowers another to represent him or act in his stead for certain purposes.

Proxy. A proxy is an authority or power to do a certain thing.

Petition. A supplication made by an inferior to a superior having jurisdiction to grant redress.

Precedent. It is an adjudged case or decision of a court of justice, considered as furnishing an example or authority for an identical or similar case afterward arising on a similar question of law.

Prescribed. The term means prescribed by rules made by the State Government, or as the case may be, by the Central Government under the Act.

Proforma Defendants. A party may be joined as a defendant in a suit merely because his presence is necessary in order to enable the Court effectually and completely to adjudicate upon the question involved.

Rejoinder. A party answering in a suit, whether for himself or another.

Redemption. A repurchase; a buying or getting back. By mortgagor, a buying back of the legal estate after it has passed to the mortgagee.

Res Judicate. A case or suit already decided.

Restrictive Trade Practice. It means any trade practice which requires a consumer to buy, hire or avail of any goods or, as the case may be, services as a condition precedent for buying, hiring or availing of any other goods or services.

Rule Nisi. An order made by the court on motion requiring a person to show cause why he should not do some particular act, or commanding the performance of the particular art forthwith. When the rule is to show cause, it is rule nisi.

Summons Case. It means a case relating to an offence, and not being a warrant case.

Tax. A tax is the compulsory exaction of money by public authority for public purposes enforceable by law. Tax is levied as part of a common burden.

Title. 'Title' is the means whereby a person's right to property is established.

Trade Mark. A mark secured by legal registration used by a manufacturer or trader to distinguish his goods from the goods of other concerns.

Ultra Vires. Beyond the powers, said of a company or corporation when exceeding the authority given to it by an Act of Parliament.

Vexatious. This means causing or likely cause vexation, the action of troubling or harassing by aggression or interference.

Warrant Case. This means a case relating to an offence punishable with death, imprisonment for life or imprisonment for a term exceeding two years.

Warranty. Guarantee or security that goods are of the quality stated. A promise or covenant by deed by the bargainer, for himself and his heirs, to warrant or secure the bargainee and his heirs, against all men for the enjoying of the thing granted.

Note

10

Illustrations

"In the strange heat all litigation brings to bear on things, the very process of litigation fosters the most profound misunderstandings in the world."

Renata Adler

Following are a few illustrations of case law relevant to the spheres of HRD, production, marketing and finance where legal interpretation or judicial intervention significantly affected the corporate activity in that sector.

Human Resource Development

1. To direct the State that in a match factory :-

   (a) Each employee should be insured and given facilities for recreation and medical attention.

   (b) Child employees should not be employed in any work connected with the manufacturing process, and should be given at less 60% of the minimum wages prescribed for an adult employee.

   (Mehta V State of TN; AIR 1991 SC 417)

   (c) Following industries were identified for priority action to counter hazardous employment of child labours.

(i)	Match making	-	Sivakasi (Tamil Nadu)
(ii)	Diamond Polishing	-	Surat (Gujarat)
(iii)	Precious Stone Polishing	-	Jaipur (Rajasthan
(iv)	Glass	-	Firozabad (Uttar Pradesh)
(v)	Brass-ware	-	Moradabad (Uttar Pradesh)
(vi)	Handmade Carpet	-	Mirzapur (Uttar Pradesh)
(vii)	Lock making	-	Aligarh (Uttar Pradesh)
(viii)	Slate	-	Markapur(Andhra Pradesh)
			Mandasaur (Madhya Pradesh)

(d) Transportation Industry. In Ram Kumar Misra V State of Bihar; AIR 1984 SC 537; the Court held that the Minimum Wages Act is applicable for ferries in Bihar and suitable directions were given. The situation involving a challenge to enhancement of dock permit fee relating to vehicles operating inside dock area was confronted in Sand Carriers Owners Union V Board of Trustees for the Port of Calcutta; AIR 1990 Cal 176.

(e) Hot Mix Plants. The rights and benefits of the workmen employed in 43 Hot Mix Plants ordered to be shifted and re-located out of Delhi were gone into in MC Mehta V Union of India; 1997(1) Scale (SP) 31.

(f) Mines and Asbestos Industries. In consumer Education and Research Centre V Union of India, AIR 1994 SC 922, the Court issued major directions to protect health of workers in mines and asbestos industry.

(g) Sexual Harassment at Work Place. The Apex Court issued guidelines having far reaching implications in Vishaka V State of Rajasthan; AIR 1997 SC 3011 aimed at prevention of sexual harassment of women at work places.

Production

(a) Flour Mill. The complaint highlighted deficiency in service because of delay in release of electric connection for running a flour mill. It was held that when the complainant had applied for electric connection, he had services for consideration and can file complaint for damage for deficiency in service. Shamsher Khan V Rajasthan State Electricity Board (1993) 2 CPR 6 (Raj).

(b) Bhopal Gas Leak Disaster Case. The Supreme Court framed an interim relief scheme and directed the Govt of Madhya Pradesh to implement it. Bhopal Gas Re-edit V UOI; AIR 1989 SC 1069.

(c) Disposal of Solid Waste. The Supreme Court issued direction to the Municipalities in the State of Uttar Pradesh to submit proposals to affect control and prevention of water pollution within six months to the Board constituted under the Water (Prevention and Control of Pollution) Act, 1974. The Court thought it appropriate to issue certain directions to be complied by the State and appoint a monitoring committee which can look into the effective functioning of the several public authorities who are responsible for the supply of drinking water, providing sewerage and providing adequate measures for disposal of solid waste. The Court took into account the interests of large number of tourists, not only from within the country but also from different foreign countries. DK Joshi V Chief Secretary, State of UP; AIR 2000 SC 384.

(d) Power Generation Industry. Directions were given by the Supreme Court to safeguard the interest of Adivasis and BCs occupying the land when forest land was sought to be acquired for construction of a super thermal plant. Banwasi Seva Ashram V State of U.P; AIR 1992 SC 921.

(e) Advertising Agency. In the case of advertising agency which was a commercial concern engaged in arranging advertisement through radio and television for a consideration of 15% such a commission was hiring service for consideration and therefore held to be a 'consumer of service'. AS Films V Bhatia Sehgal Construction Corporation; (1992) 1 CPR 288 (Delhi).

(f) Entertainment Industry. The court examined the locus-standi of proprietor of a cinema theatre to challenge the grant of no objection certificate to the rival trader. Jasbhai Mottibhai Desai V Roshan Kumar; AIR 1976 SC 578. In Girish Gandhi V Union of India; AIR 1989 SC 206; the matter related to Section 64 of the Copy Right Act with regard to an owner of video parlour.

(g) Transportation Industry. The court expressed its opinion on locus-standi of employees of APSRTC in the case of grant of stage carriage permits to private operators; APSRTC V State Transport Appellate Tribunal; AIR 1996 SC 1664.

(h) Construction Industry. The court dwelt on the matter of demolition of unauthorized construction and claim of compensation; Dalit Singh Dalal V Union of India; AIR 1997 SC 1367.

(j) Alcohol Industry. Non compliance with the provisions of law by a Unit manufacturing alcohol in Pondicherry came up before the Court in the Indian Council for Enviro Legal Action V Union of India; 1996(5) SCC 291.

(k) Pharmaceutical Industry. The Apex Court dealt with a

case involving a prayer for banning of harmful drugs and grant of compensation to the victims. Vincent V Union of India; 1989 (2) SCC 165.

(l) Meat Processing Unit. The matter concerning establishment of a meat processing unit came up before the Court in Satyavani V AP Pollution Control Board; AIR 1993 AP 257.

(m) Agro Chemicals. Where the purchaser bought some machinery for the manufacture of Dietho Dibenzoic Acid in Gujarat which it intended to carry on to earn large profits; it was held that the machinery had been purchased for commercial purpose and consequently the complainant company was not a 'consumer' under the CP Act. Abbey Chemicals(P) Ltd; Vieantibhai D Patel; (1993) 2 CPR 158 (NCDRC).

Marketing

(a) Petroleum Industry. The matter was related to allotment of Petrol Pumps. It discussed the situation where common cause, a registered society initiated a public interest litigation to expose allotments made by a Minister relating to petrol pumps out of the discretionary quota. Common Cause, a Registered Society V Union of India, AIR 1999 SC 2979.

(b) Publishing Trade. Where a publishing House had not submitted any books for selection, the Court held that it could not question the selection of list of books by Assessment Sub-Committee on the grounds of bias. J Mohapatra & Co V State of Orissa; AIR 1984 SC 1572. Another illustrative case is of M/s Book Centre and another V Mahama Gandhi University, Kottayam,

AIR 1999 Ker 60. Where an offset printing machine was admitted to have been purchased for the purpose of its use in a printing press, which was a commercial establishment; the National Commission held that the goods obtained for commercial purpose have specifically been excluded from the scope of the term of 'consumer' under the Consumer Protection Act; Oswal Fine Arts V HMT Madras; (1991)) 1 CPR 1 (NCDRC).

(c) Education Sector. The case related to management of a private school and was discussed in Pratap Kishore Misra V State of Orissa; AIR 1988 Ori 273.

(d) Tobacco Industry. The ruling given in K. Ramakrishnan V State of Kerala, AIR 1999 Ker 388; would have directly affected the sale of cigarettes to a considerable extent.

(e) Liquor Sale. The view taken by the Court with regard to prohibition would significantly remain relevant as shown in Krishna Bhat V Union of India; 1990(3) SCC 65.

(f) Glass Studio. A supplier of goods is not a consumer under the Consumer Protection Act. Glass Studio V Collector of Central Excise; (1991) II CPJ 585 (Orissa CDRC).

Finance

(a) Fertilizer Industry. A petition filed challenging the legality of sale of certain plants and equipment in the factory was decided in Fertilizer Corporation Kamager Union, Sidri V Union of India; AIR 1981 SC 344.

(b) Handloom Industry. The implications for grant of permission to hold handloom and handicraft exhibition on open ground were gone into by the Court in Citizen Council Jamshedpur V State of Bihar; AIR 1999 Pat 1.

(c) Mining Industry. A public interest litigation against illegal mining was taken up by the Court in Rural Litigation and Entitlement Kendra V State of U.P.; AIR 1988 SC 2187. A situation involving non calling of global tenders for transfer of superior quality iron ore to private sector was discussed in Dr BL Wadhera V Union of India; AIR 1998 Del 436.

(d) Liquor Trade. The right of the residents of a locality to challenge the grant of licence for running bar and restaurant under the Karnataka Excise Act in Nirmala V State of Karnataka; 1979(6) KLD 659.

(e) Load Carriers. Directions issued by the Apex Court in MC Mehta V Union of India, 1997(8) SCC 770; would continue to be relied upon in the cases of running of heavy, medium transport and light good vehicles on the roads of NCR and NCT, Delhi.

(f) Transportation Industry. The decision of the Apex Court in Virendra Singh Negi V State of U.P., (2000) 10 SCC 299. is of interest with regard to the safety of passengers of vehicles plying in hilly areas. When a jeep is engaged for transportation of passengers for hills, it can safely be held that it is used for a commercial purpose. Smt. Pushpa Meena V Shah Enterprises (Rajasthan) Ltd; (1991) 1 CPR 229 (Raj).

(g) Mutual Fund. The share means a share in the capital. The object of issuing the same is for building up capital. To raise capital, means making arrangements for carrying

Note

11

Further Study

"(Law is) an odd profession that presents its greatest scholarship in student run publications."

Morton J Horwitz, American educator

1. **The students will be well advised to familiarize themselves with the purpose and contents of under mentioned enactments.**
2. **Intellectual Property and Cyber Law**
   - (a) The Copy Right Act, 1957.
   - (b) The Designs Act, 2000.
   - (c) The Geographical Indications of Goods (Registration and Protection) Act, 1999.
   - (d) The Information Technology Act, 2000.
   - (e) The Patents Act, 1970.
   - (f) The Trade Marks Act, 1999.
   - (g) The Freedom of Information Act, 2002.

3. **Environmental Law**
   (a) The Air (Prevention and Control of Pollution) Act, 1981.
   (b) The Environment (Protection) Act, 1986.
   (c) The Public Liability Insurance Act, 1991.
   (d) The Water (Prevention and Control of Pollution) Act, 1974.
   (e) The Forest (Conservation) Act, 1980.
   (f) The Wild Lift (Protection) Act, 1972.
   (g) The Bio Diversity Act, 2002

4. **Labour Laws**
   (a) The Employees' Provident Funds and Miscellaneous Provisions Act, 1952.
   (b) The Employees State Insurance Act, 1948.
   (c) The Factories Act, 1948.
   (d) The Industrial Disputes Act, 1947.
   (e) The Minimum Wages Act, 1948.
   (f) The Payment of Bonus Act, 1965.
   (g) The Payment of Gratuity Act, 1972.

5. **Direct and Indirect Tax Law**
   (a) The Income Tax Act, 1961.
   (b) The Wealth Tax Act, 1957.
   (c) The Gift Tax Act, 1958.
   (d) The Customs Act, 1962.
   (e) The Central Excise Act, 1944.

6. Other New Legislations

(a) Competition Act 2002.

(b) Prevention of Money Laundering Act, 2002.

(c) Electricity Act, 2003.

Conclusion

A successful manager has to be aware of the basic legal provisions to effectively counter problems that may be faced by him. A common sense approach may be useful to understand and interpret legal provisions. Legal opinion and assistance should be sought at the appropriate stage from competent lawyers of known integrity.

Note

Part II

Note

12

The Information Technology Act, 2000

(No. 21 OF 2000)
[*9th June,* 2000]

An Act to provide legal recognition for transactions carried out by means of electronic data interchange and other means of electronic communication, commonly referred to as "electronic commerce", which involve the use of alternatives to paper-based methods of communication and storage of information, to facilitate electronic filing of documents with the Government agencies and further to amend the Indian Penal Code, the Indian Evidence Act, 1872, the Bankers' Books Evidence Act, 1891 and the Reserve Bank of India Act, 1934 and for matters connected therewith or incidental thereto.

WHEREAS the General Assembly of the United Nations by resolution A/RES/51/162, dated 30th January, 1997 has adopted the Model Law on Electronic Commerce adopted by the United Nations Commission on International Trade Law;

AND WHEREAS the said resolution recommends *inter alia* that all States give favourable consideration to the said Model Law when they enact or revise their laws, in view of the need for uniformity of the law applicable to alternatives to paper-based methods of communication and storage of information;

AND WHEREAS it is considered necessary to give effect to the said resolution and to promote efficient delivery of Government services by means of reliable electronic records;

BE it enacted by Parliament in the Fifty-first Year of the Republic of India as follows:—

Chapter 1

Preliminary

1. Short title, extent, commencement and application.—(1) This Act may be called the Information Technology Act, 2000.

(2) It shall extend to the whole of India and, save as otherwise provided in this Act, it applies also to any offence or contravention thereunder committed outside India by any person.

(3) It shall come into force on such date[1] as the Central Government may, by notification, appoint and different dates may be appointed for different provisions of this Act and any reference in any such provision to the commencement of this Act shall be construed as a reference to the commencement of that provision.

(4) Nothing in this Act shall apply to—

[2][(a) a negotiable instrument (other than a cheque) as defined in section 13 of the Negotiable Instruments Act,1881; (26 of 1881);]

(b) a power-of-attorney as defined in section 1A of the Powers-of-Attorney Act, 1882; (7 of 1882);]

(c) a trust as defined in section 3 of the Indian Trusts Act, 1882; (2 of 1882);]

(d) a will as defined in clause (h) of section (2) of the Indian Succession Act, 1925 (39 of 1925), including any other testamentary disposition by whatever name called;

(e) any contract for the sale or conveyance of immovable property or any interest in such property;

---

1. Came into force on 17th October,, 2000 vide G.S.R. 788 (E) dated 17th October, 2000.
2. Subs by Act 55 of 2002, sec. 12, for clause "(a) a negotiable instrument as defined in section 13 of the Negotiable Instruments Acts, 1881 (26 of 1881);" (w.e.f. 6-2-2003).

(f) any such class of documents or transactions as may be notified by the Central Government in the Official Gazette.

2. Definitions.—(1) In this Act, unless the context otherwise requires, —

(a) "access" with its grammatical variations and cognate expressions means gaining entry into, instructing or communicating with the logical, arithmetical, or memory function resources of a computer, computer system or computer network;

(b) "addressee" means a person who is intended by the originator to receive the electronic record but does not include any intermediary;

(c) "adjudicating officer" means an adjudicating officer appointed under sub-section (1) of section 46;

(d) "affixing digital signature" with its grammatical variations and cognate expressions means adoption of any methodology or procedure by a person for the purpose of authenticating an electronic record by means of digital signature;

(e) "appropriate Government" means as respects any matter,—

(i) enumerated in List II of the Seventh Schedule to the Constitution;

(ii) relating to any State law enacted under List III of the Seventh Schedule to the Constitution,

the State Government and in any other case, the Central Government;

(f) "asymmetric crypto system" means a system of a secure key pair consisting of a private key for creating a digital signature and a public key to verify the digital signature;

(g) "Certifying Authority" means a person who has been granted a licence to issue a Digital Signature Certificate under section 24;

(h) "certification practice statement" means a statement issued by a Certifying Authority to specify the practices that the Certifying Authority employs in issuing Digital Signature Certificates;

(i) "computer" means any electronic, magnetic, optical or other high-speed data processing device or system which performs logical, arithmetic, and memory functions by manipulations of electronic, magnetic or optical impulses, and includes all input, output, processing, storage, computer software, or communication facilities which are connected or related to the computer in a computer system or computer network;

(j) "computer network" means the interconnection of one or more computers through—

(i) the use of satellite, microwave, terrestrial line or other communication media; and

(ii) terminals or a complex consisting of two or more interconnected computers whether or not the interconnection is continuously maintained;

(k) "computer resource" means computer, computer system, computer network, data,computer data base or software;

(l) "computer system" means a device or collection of devices, including input and output support devices and excluding calculators which are not programmable and capable of being used in conjunction with external files, which contain computer programmes, electronic instructions, input data and output data, that performs logic, arithmetic, data storage and retrieval, communication control and other functions;

(m) "Controller" means the Controller of Certifying Authorities appointed under sub-section (l) of section 17;

(n) "Cyber Appellate Tribunal" means the Cyber Regulations Appellate Tribunal established under sub-section (1) of section 48;

(o) "data" means a representation of information, knowledge, facts, concepts or instructions which are being prepared or have been prepared in a formalised manner, and is intended to be processed, is being processed or has been processed in a computer system or computer network, and may be in any form (including computer printouts magnetic or optical storage media, punched cards, punched tapes) or stored internally in the memory of the computer;

(p) "digital signature" means authentication of any electronic record by a subscriber by means of an electronic method or procedure in accordance with the provisions of section 3;

(q) "Digital Signature Certificate" means a Digital Signature Certificate issued under subsection *(4)* of section 35;

(r) "electronic form" with reference to information means any information generated, sent, received or stored in media, magnetic, optical, computer memory, micro film, computer generated micro fiche or similar device;

(s) "Electronic Gazette" means the Official Gazette published in the electronic form;

(t) "electronic record" means data, record or data generated, image or sound stored, received or sent in an electronic form or micro film or computer generated micro fiche;

(u) "function", in relation to a computer, includes logic, control, arithmetical process, deletion, storage and retrieval and communication or telecommunication from or within a computer;

(v) "information" includes data, text, images, sound, voice, codes, computer programmes, software and data bases or micro film or computer generated micro fiche;

(w) "intermediary" with respect to any particular electronic message, means any person who on behalf of another person receives, stores or transmits that message or provides any service with respect to that message;

(x) "key pair", in an asymmetric crypto system, means a private key and its mathematically related public key, which are so related that the public key can verify a digital signature created by the private key;

(y) "law" includes any Act of Parliament or of a State Legislature, Ordinances promulgated by the President or a Governor, as the case may be. Regulations made by the President under article 240, Bills enacted as President's Act under sub-clause (a) of clause (1) of article 357 of the Constitution and includes rules, regulations, bye laws and orders issued or made there under;

(z) "licence" means a licence granted to a Certifying Authority under section 24;

(za) "originator" means a person who sends, generates, stores or transmits any electronic message; or causes any electronic message to be sent, generated, stored or transmitted to any other person but does not include an intermediary;

(zb) "prescribed" means prescribed by rules made under this Act;

(zc) "private key" means the key of a key pair used to create a digital signature;

(zd) "public key" means the key of a key pair used to verify a digital signature and listed in the Digital Signature Certificate;

(ze) "secure system" means computer hardware, software, and procedure that—

(a) are reasonably secure from unauthorised access and misuse;

(b) provide a reasonable level of reliability and correct operation;

(c) are reasonably suited to performing the intended functions; and

(d) adhere to generally accepted security procedures;

(zf) "security procedure" means the security procedure prescribed under section 16 by the Central Government;

(zg) "subscriber" means a person in whose name the Digital Signature Certificate is issued;

(zh) "verify" in relation to a digital signature, electronic record or public key, with its grammatical variations and cognate expressions, means to determine whether—

(a) the initial electronic record was affixed with the digital signature by the use of private key corresponding to the public key of the subscriber;

(b) the initial electronic record is retained intact or has been altered since such electronic record was so affixed with the digital signature.

(2) Any reference in this Act to any enactment or any provision thereof shall, in relation to an area in which such enactment or such provision is not in force, be construed as a reference to the corresponding law or the relevant provision of the corresponding law, if any, in force in that area.

Chapter II

Digital Signature

3. Authentication of electronic records. (1) Subject to the provisions of this section, any subscriber may authenticate an electronic record by affixing his digital signature.

(2) The authentication of the electronic record shall be effected by the use of asymmetric crypto system and hash function which envelop and transform the initial electronic record into another electronic record.

Explanation.—For the purposes of this sub-section, "hash function" means an algorithm mapping or translation of one sequence of bits into another, generally smaller, set known'as "hash result" such that an electronic record yields the same hash result every time the algorithm is executed with the same electronic record as its input making it computationally infeasible—

(a) to derive or reconstruct the original electronic record from the hash result produced by the algorithm;

(b) that two electronic records can produce the same hash result using the algorithm.

(3) Any person by the use of a public key of the subscriber can verify the electronic record.

(4) The private key and the public key are unique to the subscriber and constitute a functioning key pair.

Chapter III

Electronic Governance

4. Legal recognition of electronic records.—Where any law provides that information or any other matter shall be in writing or in the typewritten or printed form, then, notwithstanding anything contained in such law, such requirement shall be deemed to have been satisfied if such information or matter is—

(a) rendered or made available in an electronic form; and

(b) accessible so as to be usable for a subsequent reference.

Comments

If any information or matter is rendered or made available in an electronics form, and accessible so as to be usable for a subsequent reference, shall be deemed to have satisfied the requirement of the law which provides that information or any other matter shall be in writing or in the typewritten form.

5. Legal recognition of digital signatures.—Where any law provides that information or any other matter shall be authenticated by affixing the signature or any document shall be signed or bear the signature of any person (then, notwithstanding anything contained in such law, such requirement shall be deemed to have been satisfied, if such information or matter is authenticated by means of digital signature affixed in such manner as may be prescribed by the Central Government.

Explanation.—For the purposes of this section, "signed", with its grammatical variations and cognate expressions, shall, with reference to a person, mean affixing of his hand written signature or any mark on any document and the expression "signature" shall be construed accordingly.

Comments

If any information or any other matter is required by law to be authenticated by affixing the signature, then such requirement shall be deemed to have been satisfied if such information or matter is authenticated by means of digital signature affixed in the prescribed manner.

6. Use of electronic records and digital signatures in Government and its agencies.—(1) Where any law provides for—

(a) the filing of any form. application or any other document with any office, authority, body or agency owned or controlled by the appropriate Government in a particular manner;

(b) the issue or grant of any licence, permit, sanction or approval by whatever name called in a particular manner;

(c) the receipt or payment of money in a particular manner,

then, notwithstanding anything contained in any other law for the time being in force, such requirement shall be deemed to have been satisfied if such filing, issue, grant, receipt or payment, as the case may be, is effected by means of such electronic form as may be prescribed by the appropriate Government.

(2) The appropriate Government may, for the purposes of sub-section (1), by rules, prescribe—

(a) the manner and format in which such electronic records shall be filed, created or issued;

(b) the manner or method of payment of any fee or charges for filing, creation or issue any electronic record under clause *(a)*.

7. Retention of electronic records.—(1) Where any law provides that documents, records or information shall be retained for any specific period, then, that requirement shall be deemed to have been satisfied if such documents, records or information are retained in the electronic form, if—

(a) the information contained therein remains accessible so as to be usable for a subsequent reference;

(b) the electronic record is retained in the format in which it was originally generated, sent or received or in a format which can be demonstrated to represent accurately the information originally generated, sent or received;

(c) the details which will facilitate the identification of the origin, destination, date and time of despatch or receipt of such electronic record are available in the electronic record:

(1) Provided that this clause does not apply to any information which is automatically generated solely for the purpose of enabling an electronic record to be despatched or received.

(2) Nothing in this section shall apply to any law that expressly provides for the retention of documents, records or information in the form of electronic records.

Comments

If any law provides that documents, records or information are required to be retained for any specific period, then that requirement shall be deemed to have been satisfied if the same is retained in electronic form.

8. Publication of rule, regulation, etc., in Electronic Gazette.—Where any law provides that any rule, regulation, order, bye-law, notification or any other matter shall be published in the Official Gazette, then, such requirement shall be deemed to have been satisfied if such rule, regulation, order, bye-law, notification or any other matter is published in the Official Gazette or Electronic Gazette:

Provided that where any rule, regulation, order, byelaw, notification or any other matter is published in the Official Gazette or Electronic Gazette, the date of publication shall be deemed to be the date of the Gazette which was first published in any form.

9. Sections 6,7 and 8 not to confer right to insist document should be accepted in electronic form.— Nothing contained in sections 6, 7 and 8 shall confer a right upon any person to insist that any Ministry or Department of the Central Government or the State Government or any authority or body established by or under any law or controlled or funded by the Central or State Government should accept, issue, create, retain and preserve any document in the form of electronic records or effect any monetary transaction in the electronic form.

10. Power to make rules by Central Government in respect of digital signature.—The Central Government may, for the purposes of this Act, by rules, prescribe—

(a) the type of digital signature;

(b) the manner and format in which the digital signature shall be affixed;

(c) the manner or procedure which facilitates identification of the person affixing the digital signature;

(d) control processes and procedures to ensure adequate integrity, security and confidentiality of electronic records or payments; and

(e) any other matter which is necessary to give legal effect to digital signatures.

Chapter IV

Attribution, Acknowledgment and Despatch of Electronic Records

11. Attribution of electronic records. –An electronic record shall be attributed to the originator,—

(a) if it was sent by the originator himself;

(b) by a person who had the authority to act on behalf of the originator in respect of that electronic record; or

(c) by an information system programmed by or on behalf of the originator to operate automatically.

Comments

If any electronic record was sent by the originator himself or by a person who had the authority to act on behalf of the orginator or by an information system programmed by or on behalf of the organiser to operate automatically, then the electronic record shall be attributed to the orginator.

12. Acknowledgement of receipt.—(1) Where the originator has not agreed with the addressee that the acknowledgement of receipt of electronic record be given in a particular form or by a particular method, an acknowledgement may be given by—

(a) any communication by the addressee, automated or otherwise; or

(b) any conduct of the addressee, sufficient to indicate to the originator that the electronic record has been received.

(2) Where the originator has stipulated that the electronic record shall be binding only on receipt of an acknowledgement of such electronic record by him, then unless acknowledgement has been so received, the electronic record shall be deemed to have been never sent by the originator.

(3) Where the originator has not stipulated that the electronic record shall be binding only on receipt of such acknowledgement, and the acknowledgement has not been received by the originator within the time specified or agreed or, if no time has been specified or agreed to within a reasonable time, then the originator may give notice to the addressee stating that no acknowledgement has been received by him and specifying a reasonable time by which the acknowledgement must be received by him and if no acknowledgement is received within the aforesaid time limit he may after giving notice to the addressee, treat the electronic record as though it has never been sent.

13. Time and place of despatch and receipt of electronic record.—(1) Save as otherwise agreed to between the originator and the addressee, the dispatch of an electronic record occurs when it enters a computer resource outside the control of the originator.

(2) Save as otherwise agreed between the originator and the addressee, the time of receipt of an electronic record shall be determined as follows, namely :—

(a) if the addressee has designated a computer resource for the purpose of receiving electronic records,—

(i) receipt occurs at the time when the electronic, record enters the designated computer resource; or

(ii) if the electronic record is sent to a computer resource of the addressee that is not the designated computer resource, receipt occurs at the time when the electronic record is retrieved by the addressee;

(b) if the addressee has not designated a computer resource along with specified timings, if any, receipt occurs when the electronic record enters the computer resource of the addressee.

(3) Save as otherwise agreed to between the originator and the addressee, an electronic record is deemed to be dispatched at the place where the originator has his place of business, and is deemed to be received at the place where the addressee has his place of business.

(4) The provisions of sub-section (2) shall apply notwithstanding that the place where the computer resource is located may be different from the place where the electronic record is deemed to have been received under sub-section (3).

(5) For the purposes of this section, —

(a) if the originator or the addressee has more than one place of business, the principal place of business, shall be the place of business;

(b) if the originator or the addressee does not have a place of business, his usual place of residence shall be deemed to be the place of business;

(c) "usual place of residence", in relation to a body corporate, means the place where it is registered.

Chapter V

Secure Electronic Records and Secure Digital Signatures

14. Secure electronic record.—Where any security procedure has been applied to an electronic record at a specific point of time, then such record shall be deemed to be a secure electronic record from such point of time to the time of verification.

15. Secure digital signature.—If, by application of a security procedure agreed to by the parties concerned, it can be verified that a digital signature, at the time it was affixed, was—

(a) unique to the subscriber affixing it;

(b) capable of identifying such subscriber;

(c) created in a manner or using a means under the exclusive control of the subscriber and is linked to the electronic record to which it relates in such a manner that if the electronic record was altered the digital signature would be invalidated,

then such digital signature shall be deemed to be a secure digital signature.

Comments

If it can be verified that a digital signature at the time it was affixed, was (i) unique to the subscriber affixing it (ii) capable of identifying the subscriber, (iii) created in a manner or using a means under the exclusive control of subscriber and is linked to the electronic record to which it relates in such a manner that if the electronic record was altered the digital signature would be invalidated, then such digital signature shall be deemed to be a secure digital signature.

16. Security procedure.—The Central Government shall, for the purposes of this Act, prescribe the security procedure having regard to commercial circumstances prevailing at the time when the procedure was used, including—

(a) the nature of the transaction;

(b) the level of sophistication of the parties with reference to their technological capacity;

(c) the volume of similar transactions engaged in by other parties;

(d) the availability of alternatives offered to but rejected by any party;

(e) the cost of alternative procedures; and

(f) the procedures in general use for similar types of transactions or communications.

Chapter VI

Regulation of Certifying Authorities

17. Appointment of Controller and other officers.—(1) The Central Government may, by notification in the Official Gazette, appoint a Controller of Certifying Authorities for the purposes of this Act and may also by the same or subsequent notification appoint such number of Deputy Controllers and Assistant Controllers as it deems fit.

(2) The Controller shall discharge his functions under this Act subject to the general control and directions of the Central Government.

(3) The Deputy Controllers and Assistant Controllers shall perform the functions assigned to them by the Controller under the general superintendence and control of the Controller.

(4) The qualifications, experience and terms and conditions of service of Controller, Deputy Controllers and Assistant Controllers shall be such as may be prescribed by the Central Government.

(5) The Head Office and Branch Office of the office of the Controller shall be at such places as the Central Government may specify, and these may be established at such places as the Central Government may think fit.

(6) There shall be a seal of the Office of the Controller.

18. Functions of Controller.—The Controller may perform all or any of the following functions, namely:—

(a) exercising supervision over the activities of the Certifying Authorities;

(b) certifying public keys of the Certifying Authorities;

(c) laying down the standards to be maintained by the Certifying Authorities;

(d) specifying the qualifications and experience which employees of the Certifying Authorities should possess;

(e) specifying the conditions subject to which the Certifying Authorities shall conduct their business;

(f) specifying the contents of written, printed or visual materials and advertisements that may be distributed or used in respect of a Digital Signature Certificate and the public key;

(g) specifying the form and content of a Digital Signature Certificate and the key,

(h) specifying the form and manner in which accounts shall be maintained by the Certifying Authorities;

(i) specifying the terms and conditions subject to which auditors may be appointed and the remuneration to be paid to them;

(j) facilitating the establishment of any electronic system by a Certifying Authority either solely or jointly with other Certifying Authorities and regulation of such systems;

(k) specifying the manner in which the Certifying Authorities shall conduct their dealings with the subscribers;

(l) resolving any conflict of interests between the Certifying Authorities and the subscribers;

(m) laying down the duties of the Certifying Authorities;

(n) maintaining a data base containing the disclosure record of every Certifying Authority containing such particulars as may be specified by regulations, which shall be accessible to public.

19. Recognition of foreign Certifying Authorities.—(1) Subject to such conditions and restrictions as may be specified by regulations, the Controller may, with the previous approval of the Central Government, and by notification in the Official Gazette, recognise any foreign Certifying Authority as a Certifying Authority for the purposes of this Act.

(2) Where any Certifying Authority is recognised under sub-section (1), the Digital Signature Certificate issued by such Certifying Authority shall be valid for the purposes of this Act.

(3) The Controller may, if he is satisfied that any Certifying Authority has contravened any of the conditions and restrictions subject to which it was granted recognition under sub section (1) he may, for reasons to be recorded in writing, by notification in the Official Gazette, revoke such recognition.

20. Controller to act as repository.—(1) The Controller shall be the repository of all Digital Signature Certificates issued under this Act.

(2) The Controller shall—

(a) make use of hardware, software and procedures that are secure from intrusion and misuse;

(b) observe such other standards as may be prescribed by the Central Government,

to ensure that the secrecy and security of the digital signatures are assured.

(3) The Controller shall maintain a computerised data base of all public keys in such a manner that such data base and the public keys are available to any member of the public.

21. Licence to issue Digital Signature Certificates.—(1) Subject to the provisions of sub-section (2), any person may make an application, to the Controller, for a licence to issue Digital Signature Certificates.

(2) No licence shall be issued under sub-section (1), unless the applicant fulfills such requirements with respect to qualification, expertise, manpower, financial resources and other infrastructure facilities, which are necessary to issue Digital Signature Certificates as may be prescribed by the Central Government.

(3) A licence granted under this section shall—

(a) be valid for such period as may be prescribed by the Central Government;

(b) not be transferable or heritable;

(c) be subject to such terms and conditions as may be specified by the regulations.

22. Application for licence.—(1) Every application for issue of a licence shall be in such form as may be prescribed by the Central Government.

(2) Every application for issue of a licence shall be accompanied by

(a) a certification practice statement;

(b) a statement including the procedures with respect to identification of the applicant;

(c) payment of such fees, not exceeding twenty-five thousand rupees as may be prescribed by the Central Government;

(d) such other documents, as may be prescribed by the Central Government.

23. Renewal of licence.—An application for renewal of a licence shall be—

(a) in such form;

(b) accompanied by such fees, not exceeding five thousand rupees,

as may be prescribed by the Central Government and shall be made not less than forty-five days before the date of expiry of the period of validity of the licence.

24. Procedure for grant or rejection of licence.—The Controller may, on receipt of an application under sub-section (1) of section 21, after considering the documents accompanying the application and such other factors, as he deems fit, grant the licence or reject the application:

Provided that no application shall be rejected under this section unless the applicant has been given a reasonable opportunity of presenting his case.

25. Suspension of licence.—(1) The Controller may, if he is satisfied after making such inquiry, as he may think fit, that a Certifying Authority has,—

(a) made a statement in, or in relation to, the application for the issue or renewal of the licence, which is incorrect or false in material particulars;

(b) failed to comply with the terms and conditions subject to which the licence was granted;

[1][(c) failed to maintain the procedure and standards specified in section 30;]

(d) contravened any provisions of this Act, rule, regulation or order made thereunder,

revoke the licence:

Provided that no licence shall be revoked unless the Certifying Authority has been given a reasonable opportunity of showing cause against the proposed revocation.

(2) The Controller may, if he has reasonable cause to believe that there is any ground for revoking a licence under sub-section (1), by order, suspend such licence pending the completion of any inquiry ordered by him:

Provided that no licence shall be suspended for a period exceeding ten days unless the Certifying Authority has been given a reasonable opportunity of showing cause against the proposed suspension.

(3) No Certifying Authority whose licence has been suspended shall issue any Digital Signature Certificate during such suspension.

26. Notice of suspension or revocation of licence.—(1) Where the licence of the Certifying Authority is suspended or revoked, the Controller shall publish notice of such suspension or revocation, as the case may be, in the database maintained by him.

---

1. Subs. by S.O. 1015 (E), dated 19th September, 2002, for clause "(c) failed to maintain the standards specified under clause (b) of sub-section (2) of section 20;" (w.e.f. 19-9-2002).

(2) Where one or more repositories are specified, the Controller shall publish notices of such suspension or revocation, as the case may be, in all such repositories:

Provided that the data base containing the notice of such suspension or revocation, as the case may be, shall be made available through a web site which shall be accessible round the clock:

Provided further that the Controller may, if he considers necessary, publicise the contents of data base in such electronic or other media, as he may consider appropriate.

27. Power to delegate.—The Controller may, in writing, authorise the Deputy Controller, Assistant Controller or any officer to exercise any of the powers of the Controller under this Chapter.

28. Power to investigate contraventions.—(1) The Controller or any officer authorised by him in this behalf shall take up for investigation any contravention of the provisions of this Act, rules or regulations made there under.

(2) The Controller or any officer authorised by him in this behalf shall exercise the like powers which are conferred on Income-tax authorities under Chapter XIII of the Income-tax Act, 1961 and shall exercise such powers, subject to such limitations laid down under that Act.

29. Access to computers and data.—(1) Without prejudice to the provisions of sub-section (1) of section 68, the Controller or any person authorised by him shall, if he has reasonable cause to suspect that any contravention of the provisions of this Act, rules or regulations made thereunder has been committed, have access to any computer system, any apparatus, data or any other material connected with such system, for the purpose of searching or causing a search to be made for obtaining any information or data contained in or available to such computer system.

(2) For the purposes of sub-section (1), the Controller or any person authorised by him may, by order, direct any person incharge of, or otherwise concerned with the operation of, the computer system, data apparatus or material, to provide him

with such reasonable technical and other assistance as he may consider necessary.

30. Certifying Authority to follow certain procedures.—Every Certifying Authority shall, —

(a) make use of hardware, software and procedures that are secure from intrusion and misuse;

(b) provide a reasonable level of reliability in its services which are reasonably suited to the performance of intended functions;

(c) adhere to security procedures to ensure that the secrecy and privacy of the digital signatures are assured; and

(d) observe such other standards as may be specified by regulations.

31. Certifying Authority to ensure compliance of the Act, etc.—Every Certifying Authority shall ensure that every person employed or otherwise engaged by it complies, in the course of his employment or engagement, with the provisions of this Act, rules, regulations or orders made thereunder.

32. Display of licence.—Every Certifying Authority shall display its licence at a conspicuous place of the premises in which it carries on its business.

33. Surrender of licence.—(1) Every Certifying Authority whose licence is suspended or revoked shall immediately after such suspension or revocation, surrender the licence to the Controller.

(2) Where any Certifying Authority fails to surrender a licence under sub-section (1), the person in whose favour a licence is issued, shall be guilty of an offence and shall be punished with imprisonment which may extend up to six months or a fine which may extend up to ten thousand rupees or with both.

34. Disclosure.—(1) Every Certifying Authority shall disclose in the manner specified by regulations—

(a) its Digital Signature Certificate which contains the public key corresponding to the private key used by that Certifying Authority to digitally sign another Digital Signature Certificate;

(b) any certification practice statement relevant thereto;

(c) notice of the revocation or suspension of its Certifying Authority certificate, if any; and

(d) any other fact that materially and adversely affects either the reliability of a Digital Signature Certificate, which that Authority has issued, or the Authority's ability to perform its services.

(2) Where in the opinion of the Certifying Authority any event has occurred or any situation has arisen which may materially and adversely affect the integrity of its computer system or the conditions subject to which a Digital Signature Certificate was granted, then, the Certifying Authority shall—

(a) use reasonable efforts to notify any person who is likely to be affected by that occurrence; or

(b) act in accordance with the procedure specified in its certification practice statement to deal with such event or situation.

Chapter VII

Digital Signature Certificates

35. Certifying Authority to issue Digital Signature Certificate.—(1) Any person may make an application to the Certifying Authority for the issue of a Digital Signature Certificate in such form as may be prescribed by the Central Government

(2) Every such application shall be accompanied by such fee not exceeding twenty-five thousand rupees as may be prescribed by the Central Government, to be paid to the Certifying Authority:

Provided that while prescribing fees under sub-section (2) different fees may be prescribed for different classes of applicants.

(3) Every such application shall be accompanied by a certification practice statement or where there is no such statement, a statement containing such particulars, as may be specified by regulations.

(4) On receipt of an application under sub-section (1), the Certifying Authority may, after consideration of the certification practice statement or the other statement under subsection (3) and after making such enquiries as it may deem fit, grant the Digital Signature Certificate or for reasons to be recorded in writing, reject the application:

Provided that no Digital Signature Certificate shall be granted unless the Certifying Authority is satisfied that—

(a) the applicant holds the private key corresponding to the public key to be listed in the Digital Signature Certificate;

(b) the applicant holds a private key, which is capable of creating a digital signature;

(c) the public key to be listed in the certificate can be used to verify a digital signature affixed by the private key held by the applicant:

Provided further that no application shall be rejected unless the applicant has been given a reasonable opportunity of showing cause against the proposed rejection.

Comments

Any person can make an application to the Certifying Authority for the issue of a Digital Signature Certificate by paying the prescribed fee. Application must be accompained by a certification practice statement or a statement containing specified particulars.

36. Representations upon issuance of Digital Signature Certificate.—A Certifying Authority while issuing a Digital Signature Certificate shall certify that—

(a) it has complied with the provisions of this Act and the rules and regulations made thereunder;

(b) it has published the Digital Signature Certificate or otherwise made it available to such person relying on it and the subscriber has accepted it;

(c) the subscriber holds the private key corresponding to the public key, listed in the Digital Signature Certificate;

(d) the subscriber's public key and private key constitute a functioning key pair,

(e) the information contained in the Digital Signature Certificate is accurate; and

(f) it has no knowledge of any material fact, which if it had been included in the Digital Signature Certificate would adversely affect the reliability of the representations in clauses (a) to (d).

37. Suspension of Digital Signature Certificate.—(1) Subject to the provisions of sub-section (2), the Certifying Authority which has issued a Digital Signature Certificate may suspend such Digital Signature Certificate,—

(a) on receipt of **a request** to that effect from—

(i) the subscriber listed in the Digital Signature Certificate; or

(ii) any person duly authorised to act on behalf of that subscriber;

(b) if it is of opinion that the Digital Signature Certificate should be suspended in public interest.

(2) A Digital Signature Certificate shall not be suspended for a period exceeding fifteen days unless the subscriber has been given an opportunity of being heard in the matter.

(3) On suspension of a Digital Signature Certificate under this section, the Certifying Authority shall communicate the same to the subscriber.

38. Revocation of Digital Signature Certificate.—(1) A Certifying Authority may revoke a Digital Signature Certificate issued by it—

(a) where the subscriber or any other person authorised by him makes a request to that effect; or

(b) upon the death of the subscriber; or

(c) upon the dissolution of the firm or winding up of the company where the subscriber is a firm or a company.

(2) Subject to the provisions of sub-section (3) and without prejudice to the provisions of sub-section (1), a Certifying Authority may revoke a Digital Signature Certificate which has been issued by it at any time, if it is of opinion that—

(a) a material fact represented in the Digital Signature Certificate is false or has been concealed;

(b) a requirement for issuance of the Digital Signature Certificate was not satisfied;

(c) the Certifying Authority's private key or security system was compromised in a manner materially affecting the Digital Signature Certificate's reliability;

(d) the subscriber has been declared insolvent or dead or where a subscriber is a firm or a company, which has been dissolved, wound-up or otherwise ceased to exist

(3) A Digital Signature Certificate shall not be revoked unless the subscriber has been given an opportunity of being heard in the matter.

(4) On revocation of a Digital Signature Certificate under this section, the Certifying Authority shall communicate the same to the subscriber.

Comments

A Digital Signature Certificate issued by a Certifying Authority can be revoked if the subscriber or any person authorised by him make a request to that effect; or upon the death of the subscriber; or upon the dissolution of the firm or company where the subscriber is a firm or a company. Certifying Authority can also revoke a Digital Signature Certificate which has been issued by it if is of opinion that (i) a material fact represented in the Digital Signature Certificate is false or has been concealed, (ii) a requirement for issuance of the Digital Signature Certificate was not satisfied, (iii) the Certifying Authority's private key or security system was comprised in a manner materially affecting the Digital Signature Certificate's reliabilty, (iv) the subscriber has been declared insolvent or where a subscriber is a firm or a company which has been dissolved, wound-up or otherwise ceased to exist.

39. Notice of suspension or revocation.—(1) Where a Digital Signature Certificate is suspended or revoked under section 37 or section 38, the Certifying Authority shall publish a notice of such suspension or revocation, as the case may be, in the repository specified in the Digital Signature Certificate for publication of such notice.

(2) Where one or more repositories are specified, the Certifying Authority shall publish notices of such suspension or revocation, as the case may be in all such repositories.

Chapter VIII

Duties of Subscribers

40. Generating key pair.—Where any Digital Signature Certificate, the public key of which corresponds to the private key of that subscriber which is to be listed in the Digital Signature Certificate has been accepted by a subscriber, [1][***] the subscriber shall generate [2][that key] pair by applying the security procedure.

41. Acceptance of Digital Signature Certificate.—(1) A subscriber shall be deemed to have accepted a Digital Signature Certificate if he publishes or authorises the publication of a Digital Signature Certificate—

(a) to one or more persons;

(b) in a repository; or

otherwise demonstrates his approval of the Digital Signature Certificate in any manner.

(2) By accepting a Digital Signature Certificate the subscriber certifies to all who reasonably rely on the information contained in the Digital Signature Certificate that—

(a) the subscriber holds the private key corresponding to the public key listed in the Digital Signature Certificate and is entitled to hold the same;

1. The word "then" omitted by S.O. 1015 (E), dated 19th September, 2002 (w.e.f. 19-9-2002).
2. Subs. by S.O. 1015 (E) dated 19th September, 2002, for "the key" (w.e.f. 19-9-2002).

(b) all representations made by the subscriber to the Certifying Authority and all material relevant to the information contained in the Digital Signature Certificate are true;

(c) all information in the Digital Signature Certificate that is within the knowledge of the subscriber is true.

42. Control of private key.—(1) Every subscriber shall exercise reasonable care to retain control of the private key corresponding to the public key listed in his Digital Signature Certificate and take all steps to prevent its disclosure[3] [***].

(2) If the private key corresponding to the public key listed in the Digital Signature Certificate has been compromised, then, the subscriber shall communicate the same without any delay to the Certifying Authority in such manner as may be specified by .the regulations.

Explanation.— For the removal of doubts, it is hereby declared that the subscriber shall be liable till he has informed the Certifying Authority that the private key has been compromised.

Chapter IX

Penalties and Adjudication

43. Penalty for damage to computer, computer system, etc.—If any person without permission of the owner or any other person who is incharge of a computer, computer system or computer network,—

(a) accesses or secures access to such computer, computer system or computer network;

(b) downloads, copies or extracts any data, computer data base or information from such computer, computer system or computer network including information or data held or stored in any removable storage medium;

3. The word "to a person not auhtorised to affix the digital signature of the subscriber" omitted by S.O. 1015 (E) , dated 19th Septemcer, 2002 (w.e.f. 19-9-2002).

(c) introduces or causes to be introduced any computer contaminant or computer virus into any computer, computer system or computer network;

(d) damages or causes to be damaged any computer, computer system or computer network, data, computer data base or any other programmes residing in such computer, computer system or computer network;

(e) disrupts or causes disruption of any computer, computer system or computer network;

(f) denies or causes the denial of access to any person authorised to access any computer, computer system or computer network by any means;

(g) provides any assistance to any person to facilitate access to a computer, computer system or computer network in contravention of the provisions of this Act, rules or regulations made thereunder;

(h) charges the services availed of by a person to the account of another person by tampering with or manipulating any computer, computer system, or computer network,

he shall be liable to pay damages by way of compensation not exceeding one crore rupees to the person so affected.

Explanation.—For the purposes of this section,—

(i) "computer contaminant" means any set of computer instructions that are designed—

(a) to modify, destroy, record, transmit data or programme residing within a computer, computer system or computer network; or

(b) by any means to usurp the normal operation of the computer, computer system, or computer network;

(ii) "computer database" means a representation of information, knowledge, facts, concepts or instructions in text, image, audio, video that are being prepared or have been prepared in a formalised manner or have been produced by a computer, computer system or computer network and are intended for use in a computer, computer system or computer network;

(iii) "computer virus" means any computer instruction, information, data or programme that destroys, damages, degrades or adversely affects the performance of a computer resource or attaches itself to another computer resource and operates when a programme, data or instruction is executed or some other event takes place in that computer resource;

(iv) "damage" means to destroy, alter, delete, add, modify or rearrange any computer resource by any means.

Comments

If any person without permission of the owner or an other person who is incharge of a computer system or computer network—(i) accesses such computer, computer system or computer network; (ii) downloads, copies or extracts any data, computer data-base or information; (iii) introduces or causes to be introduced any computer contaminant or computer virus; (iv) damaged or causes to be damaged any computer, computer system or computer network data,, computer database or any other programmes; (v) disrupts or causes disruption; (vi) denies or causes the denial of access to any person authorised to access; (vii) provides any assistance to any person to facilitate access in contravention of the account of another person by tampering with or manipulating any computer, computer system or computer network, he shall be liable to pay damages upto ten lakh rupees to the person so affected.

44. Penalty for failure to furnish information return, etc.– If any person who is required under this Act or any rules or regulations made thereunder to—

(a) furnish any document, return or report to the Controller or the Certifying Authority fails to furnish the same, he shall be liable to a penalty not exceeding one lakh and fifty thousand rupees for each such failure;

(b) file any return or furnish any information, books or other documents within the time specified therefor in the regulations fails to file return or furnish the same within the time specified therefor in the regulations, he shall be liable to a penalty not exceeding five thousand rupees for every day during which such failure continues;

(c) maintain books of account or records fails to maintain the same, he shall be liable to a penalty not exceeding ten thousand rupees for every day during which the failure continues.

45. Residuary penalty.—Whoever contravenes any rules or regulations made under this Act, for the contravention of which no penalty has been separately provided, shall be liable to pay a compensation not exceeding twenty-five thousand rupees to the person affected by such contravention or a penalty not exceeding twenty-five thousand rupees.

Comments

If any person contravenes any rules or regulations made under this Act, he is liable to pay a compensation upto twenty-five thousand rupees to the person affected by such contravention.

46. Power to adjudicate.—(1) For the purpose of adjudging under this Chapter whether any person has committed a contravention of any of the provisions of this Act or of any rule, regulation, direction or order made thereunder the Central Government shall, subject to the provisions of sub-section (3), appoint any officer not below the rank of a Director to the Government of India or an equivalent officer of a State Government to be an adjudicating officer'for holding an inquiry in the manner prescribed by the Central Government.

(2) The adjudicating officer shall, after giving the person referred to in sub-section (1) a reasonable opportunity for making representation in the matter and if, on such inquiry, he is satisfied that the person has committed the contravention, he may impose such penalty or award such compensation as he thinks fit in accordance with the provisions of that section.

(3) No person shall be appointed as an adjudicating officer unless he possesses such experience in the field of Information Technology and legal or judicial experience as may be prescribed by the Central Government.

(4) Where more than one adjudicating officers are appointed, the Central Government shall specify by order the matters and places with respect to which such officers shall exercise their jurisdiction.

(5) Every adjudicating officer shall have the powers of a civil court which are conferred oh the Cyber Appellate Tribunal under sub-section (2) of section 58, and—

(a) all proceedings before it shall be deemed to be judicial proceedings within the meaning of sections 193 and 228 of the Indian Penal Code;

(b) shall be deemed to be a civil court for the purposes of sections 345 and 346 of the Code of Criminal Procedure, 1973. (2 of 1974)

47. Factors to be taken into account by the adjudicating officer.—While adjudging the quantum of compensation under this Chapter, the adjudicating officer shall have due regard to the following factors, namely:—

(a) the amount of gain of unfair advantage, wherever quantifiable, made as a result of the default;

(b) the amount of loss caused to any person as a result of the default;

(c) the repetitive nature of the default

Chapter X

The Cyber Regulations Appellate Tribunal

48. Establishment of Cyber Appellate Tribunal.—(1) The Central Government shall, by notification, establish one or more appellate tribunals to be known as the Cyber Regulations Appellate Tribunal.

(2) The Central Government shall also specify, in the notification referred to in subsection (1), the matters and places in relation to which the Cyber Appellate Tribunal may exercise jurisdiction.

49. Composition of Cyber Appellate Tribunal.—A Cyber Appellate Tribunal shall consist of one person only (hereinafter referred to as the Presiding Officer of the Cyber Appellate Tribunal) to be appointed, by notification, by the Central Government.

50. Qualifications for appointment as Presiding Officer of the Cyber Appellate Tribunal.—A person shall not be qualified for appointment as the Presiding Officer of a Cyber Appellate Tribunal unless he—

(a) is, or has been. or is qualified to be, a Judge of a High Court; or

(b) is, or has been a member of the Indian Legal Service and is holding or has held a post in Grade I of that Service for at least three years.

51. Term of office.—The Presiding Officer of a Cyber Appellate Tribunal shall hold office for a term of five years from the date on which he enters upon his office or until he attains the age of sixty-five years, whichever is earlier.

52. Salary, allowances and other terms and conditions of service of Presiding Officer.—The salary and allowances payable to, and the other terms and conditions of service including pension, gratuity and other retirement benefits of, the Presiding Officer of a Cyber Appellate Tribunal shall be such as may be prescribed:

Provided that neither the salary and allowances nor the other terms and conditions of service of the Presiding Officers shall be varied to his disadvantage after appointment.

53. Filling up of vacancies.—If, for reason other than temporary absence, any vacancy occurs in the office of the Presiding Officer of a Cyber Appellate Tribunal, then the Central Government shall appoint another person in accordance with the provisions of this Act to fill the vacancy and the proceedings may be continued before the Cyber Appellate Tribunal from the stage at which the vacancy is filled.

54. Resignation and removal.—(1) The Presiding Officer of a Cyber Appellate Tribunal may, by notice in writing under his hand addressed to the Central Government, resign his office:

Provided that the said Presiding Officer shall, unless he is permitted by the Central Government to relinquish his office sooner, continue to hold office until the expiry of three months from the date of receipt of such notice or until a person duly appointed as his successor enters upon his office or until the expiry of his term of office, whichever is the earliest.

(2) The Presiding Officer of a Cyber Appellate Tribunal shall not be removed from his office except by an order by the Central Government on the ground of proved misbehaviour or incapacity after an inquiry made by a Judge of the Supreme Court in which the Presiding Officer concerned has been informed of the charges against him and given a reasonable opportunity of being heard in respect of these charges.

(3) The Central Government may, by rules, regulate the procedure for the investigation of misbehaviour or incapacity of the aforesaid Presiding Officer.

55. Orders constituting Appellate Tribunal to be final and not to invalidate its proceedings.—No order of the Central Government appointing any person as the Presiding Officer of a Cyber Appellate Tribunal shall be called in question in any manner and no act or proceeding before a Cyber Appellate Tribunal shall be called in question in any manner on the ground merely of any defect in the constitution of a Cyber Appellate Tribunal.

56. Staff of the Cyber Appellate Tribunal.—(1) The Central Government shall provide the Cyber Appellate Tribunal with such officers and employees as that Government may think fit.

(2) The officers and employees of the Cyber Appellate Tribunal shall discharge their functions under general superintendence of the Presiding Officer.

(3) The salaries, allowances and other conditions of service of the officers and employees of the Cyber Appellate Tribunal shall be such as may be prescribed by the Central Government.

57. Appeal to Cyber Appellate Tribunal.—(1) Save as provided in sub-section (2), any person aggrieved by an order made by controller or an adjudicating officer under this Act may prefer an appeal to a Cyber Appellate Tribunal having jurisdiction in the matter.

(2) No appeal shall lie to the Cyber Appellate Tribunal from an order made by an adjudicating officer with the consent of the parties.

(3) Every appeal under sub-section (1) shall be filed within a period of forty-five days from the date on which a copy of the order made by the Controller or the adjudicating officer is received by the person aggrieved and it shall be in such form and be accompanied by such fee as may be prescribed:

Provided that the Cyber Appellate Tribunal may entertain an appeal after the expiry of the said period of forty-five days if it is satisfied that there was sufficient cause for not filing it within that period.

(4) On receipt of an appeal under sub-section (1), the Cyber Appellate Tribunal may, after giving the parties to the appeal, an opportunity of being heard, pass such orders thereon as it thinks fit, confirming, modifying or setting aside the order appealed against.

(5) The Cyber Appellate Tribunal shall send a copy of every order made by it to the parties to the appeal and to the concerned Controller or adjudicating officer.

(6) The appeal filed before the Cyber Appellate Tribunal under sub-section (1) shall be dealt with by it as expeditiously as possible and endeavour shall be made by it to dispose of the appeal finally within six months from the date of receipt of the appeal.

58. Procedure and powers of the Cyber Appellate Tribunal.—(1) The Cyber Appellate Tribunal shall not be bound by the procedure laid down by the Code of civil Procedure, 1908, (5 of 1908), but shall be guided by the principles of natural justice and, subject to the other provisions of this Act and of any rules, the Cyber Appellate Tribunal shall have powers to regulate its own procedure including the place at which it shall have its sittings.

(2) The Cyber Appellate Tribunal shall have, for the purposes of discharging its functions under this Act, the same powers as are vested in a civil court under the Code of Civil Procedure, 1908, (5 of 1908), while trying a suit, in respect of the following matters, namely:—

(a) summoning and enforcing the attendance of any person and examining him on oath;

(b) requiring the discovery and production of documents or other electronic records;

(c) receiving evidence on affidavits;

(d) issuing commissions for the examination of witnesses or documents;

(e) reviewing its decisions;

(f) dismissing an application for default or deciding it *ex parte;*

(g) any other matter which may be prescribed.

(3) Every proceeding before the Cyber Appellate Tribunal shall be deemed to be a judicial proceeding within the meaning of sections 193 and 228, and for the purposes of section 196 of the Indian Penal Code (45 of 1860) and the Cyber Appellate Tribunal shall be deemed to be a civil court for the purposes of section 195 and Chapter XXVI of the Code of Criminal Procedure, 1973 (2 of 1974).

59. Right to legal representation.—

The appellant may either appear in person or authorise one or more legal practitioners or any of its officers to present his or its case before the Cyber Appellate Tribunal.

60. Limitation.—The provisions of the Limitation Act, 1963 (36 of 1963), shall, as far as may be, apply to an appeal made to the Cyber Appellate Tribunal.

61. Civil court not to have jurisdiction.—No court shall have jurisdiction to entertain any suit or proceeding in respect of any matter which an adjudicating officer appointed under this Act or the Cyber Appellate Tribunal constituted under this Act is empowered by or under this Act to determine and no injunction shall be granted by any court or other authority in respect of any action taken or to be taken in pursuance of any power conferred by or under this Act.

62. Appeal to High Court.—Any person aggrieved by any decision or order of the Cyber Appellate Tribunal may file an appeal to the High Court within sixty days from the date of communication of the decision or order of the Cyber Appellate Tribunal to him on any question of fact or law arising out of such order:

Provided that the High Court may, if it is satisfied that the appellant was prevented by sufficient cause from filing the appeal within the said period, allow it to be filed within a further period not exceeding sixty days.

63. Compounding of contraventions.—(1) Any contravention under this[1] [Act] may, either before or after the institution of adjudication proceedings, be compounded by the Controller or such other officer as may be specially authorised by him in this behalf or by the adjudicating officer, as the case may be, subject to such conditions as the Controller or such other officer or the adjudicating officer may specify:

Provided that such sum shall not, in any case, exceed the maximum amount of the penalty which may be imposed under this Act for the contravention so compounded.

(2) Nothing in sub-section (1) shall apply to a person who commits the same or similar contravention within a period of three years from the date on which the first contravention, committed by him, was compounded.

Explanation.—For the purposes of this sub-section, any second or subsequent contravention committed after the expiry of a period of three years from the date on which the contravention was previously compounded shall be deemed to be a first contravention.

---

1. Subs. by S.O. 1015 (E), dated 19th September, 2002,, for "Chapter" (w.e.f. 19-9-2002).

(3) Where any contravention has been compounded under sub-section (1), no proceeding or further proceeding, as the case may be, shall be taken against the person guilty of such contravention in respect of the contravention so compounded.

64. Recovery of penalty.—A penalty imposed under this Act, if it is not paid, shall be recovered as an arrear of land revenue and the licence or the Digital Signature Certificate, as the case may be, shall be suspended till the penalty is paid.

Chapter XI

Offences

65. Tampering with computer source documents.—Whoever knowingly or intentionally conceals, destroys or alters or intentionally or knowingly causes another to conceal, destroy or alter any computer source code used for a computer, computer programme, computer system or computer network, when the computer source code is required to be kept or maintained by law for the time being in force, shall be punishable with imprisonment up to three years, or with fine which may extend up to two lakh rupees, or with both.

Explanation.—For the purposes of this section, "computer source code" means the listing of programmes, computer commands, design and layout and programme analysis of computer resource in any form.

Comments

If any person knowingly or intentionally conceals, destroys code or alters or cause another to conceal, destroy or alter any computer source used for a computer, computer programme, computer system, or computer network, he shall be punishable with imprisonment upto three years, or with fine upto two lakh rupees, or with both.

66. Hacking with computer system.—(1) Whoever with the intent to cause or knowing that he is likely to cause wrongful loss or damage to the public or any person destroys or deletes or alters any information residing in a computer resource or diminishes its value or utility or affects it injuriously by any means, commits hacking:

(2) Whoever commits hacking shall be punished with imprisonment up to three years, or with fine which may extend upto two lakh rupees, or with both.

67. Publishing of information which is obscene in electronic form.—Whoever publishes or transmits or causes to be published in the electronic form, any material which is lascivious or appeals to the prurient interest or if its effect is such as to tend to deprave and corrupt persons who are likely, having regard to all relevant circumstances, to read, see or hear the matter contained or embodied in it, shall be punished on first conviction with imprisonment of either description for a term which may extend to five years and with fine which may extend to one lakh rupees and in the event of a second or subsequent conviction with imprisonment of either description for a term which may extend to ten years and also with fine which may extend to two lakh rupees.

68. Power of Controller to give directions.—(1) The Controller may, by order, direct a Certifying Authority or any employee of such Authority to take such measures or cease carrying on such activities as specified in the order if those are necessary to ensure compliance with the provisions of this Act, rules or any regulations made thereunder.

(2) Any person who fails to comply with any order under sub-section (1) shall be guilty of an offence and shall be liable on conviction to imprisonment for a term not exceeding three years or to a fine not exceeding two lakh rupees or to both.

69. Directions of Controller to a subscriber to extend facilities to decrypt information.—(1) If the Controller is satisfied that it is necessary or expedient so to do in the interest of the sovereignty or integrity of India, the security of the State, friendly relations with foreign States or public order or for preventing incitement to the commission of any cognizable offence, for reasons to be recorded in writing, by order, direct any agency of the Government to intercept any information transmitted through any computer resource.

(2) The subscriber or any person incharge of the computer resource shall, when called upon by any agency which has been directed under sub-section (1), extend all facilities and technical assistance to decrypt the information.

(3) The subscriber or any person who fails to assist the agency referred to in sub-section (2) shall be punished with an imprisonment for a term which may extend to seven years.

70. Protected system.—(1) The appropriate Government may, by notification in the Official Gazette, declare that any computer, computer system or computer network to be a protected system.

(2) The appropriate Government may, by order in writing, authorise the persons who are authorised to access protected systems notified under sub-section (1).

(3) Any person who secures access or attempts to secure access to a protected system in contravention of the provisions of this section shall be punished with imprisonment of either description for a term which may extend to ten years and shall also be liable to fine.

Comments

Any computer, computer system or computer network can be declared protected system by the Government by notificatioin. Only authorised persons can have access to the protected system. Any person who secures access or attempts to secure access to a protected system in contravention of the provision shall be punished with imprisonment upto ten years and shall also be liable to fines.

71. Penalty for misrepresentation.—Whoever makes any misrepresentation to, or suppresses any material fact from, the Controller or the Certifying Authority for obtaining any licence or Digital Signature Certificate, as the case may be. shall be punished with imprisonment for a term which may extend to two years, or with fine which may extend to one lakh rupees, or with both.

Comments

For obtaining any licence or Digital Signature Certificate if any person makes any misrepresentation or suppresses any material fact, he shall be punished with imprisonment upto two years, or with fine upto one lakh rupees, or with both.

72. Penalty for breach of confidentiality and privacy.—Save as otherwise provided in this Act or any other law for the time being in force, if any person who, in pursuance of any of the powers conferred under this Act, rules or regulations made thereunder, has secured access to any electronic record, book, register, correspondence, information, document or other material without the consent of the person concerned discloses such electronic record, book, register, correspondence, information, document or other material to any other person shall be punished with imprisonment for a term which may extend to two years, or with fine which may extend to one lakh rupees, or with both.

Comments

If any person has secured access to any electronic record, book, register, correspondence, information, document or other material without the consent of the person concernerd and discloses the same to any other person then he shall be punished with imprisonment upto two years, or with fine upto one lakh rupees, or with both.

73. Penalty for publishing Digital Signature Certificate false in certain particulars.—(1) No person shall publish a Digital Signature Certificate or otherwise make it available to any other person with the knowledge that—

(a) the Certifying Authority listed in the certificate has not issued it; or

(b) the subscriber listed in the certificate has not accepted it; or

(c) the certificate has been revoked or suspended,

unless such publication is for the purpose of verifying a digital signature created prior to such suspension or revocation.

(2) Any person who contravenes the provisions of sub-section (1) shall be punished with imprisonment for a term which may extend to two years, or with fine which may extend to one lakh rupees, or with both.

Comments

If any person publishers a Digital Signature Certificate or otherwise makes it available to any other person with the knowledge that (i) the Certifying Authority listed in the certificate has not issued it; or (ii) the subscriber listed in the certificate has not accepted it; or (iii) the certificate has been revoked or suspended unless such publication is for the purpose of verifying a digital signature created prior to such suspension or revocation, he shall be punished with imprisonment upto two years or with fine upto one lakh rupees, or with both.

74. Publication for fraudulent purpose.—Whoever knowingly creates, publishes or otherwise makes available a Digital Signature Certificate for any fraudulent or unlawful purpose shall be punished with imprisonment for a term which may extend to two years, or with fine which may extend to one lakh rupees, or with both.

Comments

If any person knowingly creates, publishes or otherwise makes available a Digital Signature Certificate for any fraudulent or unlawful purpose, he shall be punished with imprisonment upto two years, or with fine upto one lakh rupees, or with both.

75. Act to apply for offence or contravention commited outside India.—(1) Subject to the provisions of sub-section (2), the provisions of this Act shall apply also to any offence or contravention committed outside India by any person irrespective of his nationality.

(2) For the purposes of sub-section (1), this Act shall apply to an offence or contravention committed outside India by any person if the act or conduct constituting the offence or contravention involves a computer, computer system or computer network located in India.

76. Confiscation.—Any computer, computer system, floppies, compact disks, tape drives or any other accessories related thereto, in respect of which any provision of this Act. rules, orders or regulations made thereunder has been or is being contravened, shall be liable to confiscation:

Provided that where it is established to the satisfaction of the court adjudicating the confiscation that the person in whose possession, power or control of any such computer, computer system, floppies, compact disks, tape drives or any other accessories relating thereto is found is not responsible for the contravention of the provisions of this Act, rules, orders or regulations made thereunder, the court may, instead of making an order for confiscation of such computer, computer system, floppies, compact disks, tape drives or any other accessories related thereto, make such other order authorised by this Act against the person contravening of the provisions of this Act, rules, orders or regulations made thereunder as it may think fit.

77. Penalties or confiscation not to interfere with other punishments.—No penalty imposed or confiscation made under this Act shall prevent the imposition of any other punishment to which the person affected thereby is liable under any other law for the time being in force.

78. Power to investigate offences.—Notwithstanding anything contained in the Code of Criminal Procedure, 1973, (2 of 1974), a police officer not below the rank of Deputy Superintendent of Police shall investigate any offence under this Act.

Chapter XII

Network Service Providers not to be Liable in Certain Cases

79. Network service providers not to be liable in certain cases.—For the removal of doubts, it is hereby declared that no person providing any service as a network service provider shall be liable under this Act, rules or regulations made thereunder for any third party information or data made available by him if he proves that the offence or contravention was committed without his knowledge or that he had exercised all due diligence to prevent the commission of such offence or contravention.

Explanation.—For the purposes of this section, —

(a) "network service provider" means an intermediary;

(b) "third party information" means any information dealt with by a network service provider in his capacity as an intermediary;

Chapter XIII

Miscellaneous

80. Power of police officer and other officers to enter, search, etc.—(1) Notwithstanding anything contained in the Code of Criminal Procedure, 1973 (2 of 1974), any police officer, not below the rank of a Deputy Superintendent of Police, or any other officer of the Central Government or a State Government authorised by the Central Government in this behalf may enter any public place and search and arrest without warrant any person found therein who is reasonably suspected of having committed or of committing or of being about to commit any offence under this Act

Explanation.—For the purposes of this sub-section, the expression "public place" includes any public conveyance, any hotel, any shop or any other place intended for use by, or accessible to the public.

(2) Where any person is arrested under sub-section (1) by an officer other than a police officer, such officer shall, without unnecessary delay, take or send the person arrested before a magistrate having jurisdiction in the case or before the officer-in-charge of a police station.

(3) The provisions of the Code of Criminal Procedure, 1973 (2 of 1974) shall, subject to the provisions of this section, apply, so far as may be, in relation to any entry, search or arrest, made under this section.

81. Act to have overriding effect.—The provisions of this Act shall have effect notwithstanding anything inconsistent therewith contained in any other law for the time being in force.

[1][**81A. Application of the Act to electronic cheque and truncated cheque.**—

(1) The provisions of this Act, for the time being in force, shall apply to, or in relation to, electronic cheques and the truncated cheques subject to such modifications and amendments as may be necessary for carrying out the purposes of the Negotiable Instruments Act, 1881 (26 of 1881), by the Central Government, in consulatation with the Reserve Bank of India, by notification in the Official Gazette.

(2) Every notification made by the Central Government under sub-section (1) shall be laid, as soon as may be after it is made, before each House of Parliament, while it is in session, for a total period of thirty days which may be comprised in one session or in two or more successive sessions, and if, before the expiry of the session immediately following the session or the successive sessions aforesaid, both Houses agree in making any modification in the notification or both Houses agree that the notification should not be made, the notification shall thereafter have effect only in such modified form or be of no effect, as the case may be; so however, that any such modification or annulment shall be without prejudice to the validity of anything previously done under that notification.

1. Ins. by Act 55 of 2002, sec. 13 (w.e.f.6-2-2003)

Explanation.—For the purpose of this Act, the expressions "electronic cheque" and "truncated cheque" shall have the same meaning as assigned to them in section 6 of the Negotiable Instruments Act,1881 (26 of 1881).]

82. Controller, Deputy Controller and Assistant Controllers to be public servants.—The Presiding Officer and other officers and employees of a Cyber Appellate Tribunal, the Controller, the Deputy Controller and the Assistant Controllers shall be deemed to be public servants within the meaning of section 21 of the Indian Penal Code (45 of 1860).

83. Power to give directions.—The Central Government may give directions to any State Government as to the carrying into execution in the State of any of the provisions of this Act or of any rule, regulation or order made thereunder.

84. Protection of action taken in good faith.—No suit, prosecution or other legal proceeding shall lie against the Central Government, the State Government, the Controller or any person acting on behalf of him, the Presiding Officer, adjudicating officers and the staff of the Cyber Appellate Tribunal for anything which is in good faith done or intended to be done in pursuance of this Act or any rule, regulation or order made thereunder.

85. Offences by companies.—(1) Where a person committing a contravention of any of the provisions of this Act or of any rule, direction or order made thereunder is a company, every person who, at the time the contravention was committed, was in charge of, and was responsible to, the company for the conduct of business of the company as well as the company, shall be guilty of the contravention and shall be liable to be proceeded against and punished accordingly:

Provided that nothing contained in this sub-section shall render any such person liable to punishment if he proves that the contravention took place without his knowledge or that he exercised all due diligence to prevent such contravention.

(2) Notwithstanding anything contained in sub-section (1), where a contravention of any of the provisions of this Act or of any rule, direction or order made thereunder has been committed

by a company and it is proved that the contravention has taken place with the consent or connivance of, or is attributable to any neglect on the part of, any director, manager, secretary or other officer of the company, such director, manager, secretary or other officer shall also be deemed to be guilty of the contravention and shall be liable to be proceeded against and punished accordingly.

Explanation.—For the purposes of this section,—

(i) "company" means any body corporate and includes a firm or other association of individuals; and

(ii) "director", in relation to a firm, means a partner in the firm.

86. Removal of difficulties.—(1) If any difficulty arises in giving effect to the provisions of this Act, the Central Government may, by order published in the Official Gazette, make such provisions not inconsistent with the provisions of this Act as appear to it to be necessary or expedient for removing the difficulty:

Provided that no order shall be made under this section after the expiry of a period of two years from the commencement of this Act.

(2) Every order made under this section shall be laid, as soon as may be after it is made, before each House of Parliament.

87. Power of Central Government to make rules.—(1) The Central Government may, by notification in the Official Gazette and in the Electronic Gazette make rules to carry out the provisions of this Act.

(2) In particular, and without prejudice to the generality of the foregoing power, such rules may provide for all or any of the following mailers, namely:—

(a) the manner in which any information or matter may be authenticated by means of digital signature under section 5;

(b) the electronic form in which filing, issue, grant or payment shall be effected under sub-section (1) of section 6;

(c) the manner and format in which electronic records shall be filed, or issued and the method of .payment under sub-section (2) of section 6;

(d) the matters relating to the type of digital signature, manner and format in which it may be affixed under section 10;

(e) the security procedure for the purpose of creating secure electronic record and secure digital signature under section 16;

(f) the qualifications, experience and terms and conditions of service of Controller, Deputy Controllers and Assistant Controllers under section 17;

(g) other standards to be observed by the Controller under clause (b) *of* subsection (2) of section 20;

(h) the requirements which an applicant must fulfill under sub-section (2) of section 21;

(i) the period of validity of licence granted under clause (a) of sub-section (3) of section 21;

(j) the form in which an application for licence may be made under sub-section (1) of section 22;

(k) the amount of fees payable under clause (c) of sub-section (2) of section 22;

(l) such other documents which shall accompany an application for licence under clause (a) of sub-section (2) of section 22;

(m) the form and the fee for renewal of a licence and the fee payable there of under section 23;

(n) the form in which application for issue of a Digital Signature Certificate may be made under sub-section (1) of section 35;

(o) the fee to be paid to the Certifying Authority for issue of a Digital Signature Certificate under sub-section (2) of section 35;

(p) the manner in which the adjudicating officer shall hold inquiry under subsection (1) of section 46;

(q) the qualification and experience which the adjudicating officer shall possess under sub-section (3) *of* section 46;

(r) the salary, allowances and the other terms and conditions of service of the Presiding Officer under section 52;

(s) the procedure for investigation of misbehaviour or incapacity of the Presiding Officer under sub-section (3) of section 54;

(t) the salary and allowances and other conditions of service of other officers and employees under sub-section (3) of section 56;

(u) the form in which appeal may be filed and the fee thereof under sub-section (3) of section 57;

(v) any other power of a civil court required to be prescribed under clause (g) of subsection (2) of section 58; and

(w) any other matter which is required to be, or may be, prescribed.

(3) Every notification made by the Central Government under clause (f) of sub-section (4) of section 1 and every rule made by it shall be laid, as soon as may be after it is made, before each House of Parliament, while it is in session, for a total period of thirty days which may be comprised in one session or in two or more successive sessions, and if, before the expiry of the session immediately following the session or the successive sessions aforesaid, both Houses agree in making any modification in the notification or the rule or both Houses agree that the notification or the rule should not be made, the notification or the rule shall thereafter have effect only in such modified form or be of no effect, as the case may be; so, however, that any such modification or annulment shall be without prejudice to the validity of anything previously done under that notification or rule.

88. Constitution of Advisory Committee.—(1) The Central Government shall, as soon as may be after the commencement of this Act, constitute a Committee called the Cyber Regulations Advisory Committee.

(2) The Cyber Regulations Advisory Committee shall consist of a Chairperson and such number of other official and non-official members representing the interests principally affected or having special knowledge of the subject-matter as the Central Government may deem fit.

(3)The Cyber Regulations Advisory Committee shall advise—

(a) the Central Government either generally as regards any rules or for any other purpose connected with this Act;

(b) the Controller in framing the regulations under this Act.

(4) There shall be paid to the non-official members of such Committee such travelling and other allowances as the Central Government may fix.

Comments

The Central Government has constituted the "Cyber Regulation Advisory Committee" consisting of the foillowing, namely:—

1.	Minister, Information Technology	Chairman
2.	Secretary, Legislative Department	Member
3.	Secretary, Ministry of Information Technology	Member
4.	Secretary, Department of Telecommunications	Member
5.	Finance Secetary	Member
6.	Secretary, Ministry of Defence	Member
7.	Secretary, Ministry of Home Affairs	Member
8.	Secretary, Ministry of Commerce	Member
9.	Deputy Governor, Reserve Bank of India	Member
10.	Shri T.K. Vishwanathan, presently Member Seceratry, Law Commission	Member
11.	President, NASSCOM	Member
12.	President, Internet Service Providers Association	Member
13.	Director, Central Bureau of Investigation	Member
14.	Controller of Certifying Authority	Member
15.	Information Technology Secretary by rotation from the States	Member
16.	Director-General of Police by rotation from the States	Member
17.	Director, IIT by rotation from the IITs	Member
18.	Representative of CII	Member

19.	Representative of FICCI	Member
20.	Representative of ASSOCHAM	Member
21.	Senior Director, Ministry of Information Technology	Member-Secretary

The Committee may co-opt any person as Member based on specific meetings *Vide* G.S.R. 790 (E), dated 17th October 2000.

89. Power of Controller to make regulations.—(1) The Controller may, after consultation with the Cyber Regulations Advisory Committee and with the previous approval of the Central Government, by notification in the Official Gazette, make regulations consistent with this Act and the rules made thereunder to carry out the purposes of this Act.

(2) In particular, and without prejudice to the generality of the foregoing power, such regulations may provide for all or any of the following matters, namely: —

(a) the particulars relating to maintenance of data-base containing the disclosure record of every Certifying Authority under clause[1] [(n)] of section 18;

(b) the conditions and restrictions subject to which the Controller may recognise any foreign Certifying Authority under sub-section (1) of section 19;

(c) the terms and conditions subject to which a licence may be granted under clause (c) of sub-section *(3)* of section 21;

(d) other standards to be observed by a Certifying Authority under clause (d) of section 30;

(e) the manner in which the Certifying Authority shall disclose the matters specified in sub-section (1) of section 34;

(f) the particulars of statement which shall accompany an application under sub-section (3) of section 35;

(g) the manner by which the subscriber shall communicate the compromise of private key to the certifying Authority under sub-section (2) of section 42.

1. Subs by S.O. 1015 (E), dated 19th September. 2002, for "(m)" (w.e.f. 19-9-2002).

(3) Every regulation made under this Act shall be laid, as soon as may be after it is made, before each House of Parliament, while it is in session, for a total period of thirty days which may be comprised in one session or in two or more successive sessions, and if, before the expiry of the session immediately following the session or the successive sessions aforesaid, both Houses agree in making any modification in the regulation or both Houses agree that the regulation should not be made, the regulation shall thereafter have effect only in such modified form or be of no effect, as the case may be; so, however, that any such modification or annulment shall be without prejudice to the validity of anything previously done under that regulation.

90. Power of State Government to make rules.—(1) The State Government may, by notification in the Official Gazette, make rules to carry out the provisions of this Act.

(2) In particular, and without prejudice to the generality of the foregoing power, such rules may provide for all or any of the following matters, namely: —

(a) the electronic form in which filing, issue, grant receipt or payment shall be effected under sub-section (1) of section 6;

(b) for matters specified in sub-section (2) of section 6;

(c) any other matter which is required to be provided by rules by the State Government.

(3) Every rule made by the State Government under this section shall be laid, as soon as may be after it is made, before each House of the State Legislature where it consists of two Houses, or where such Legislature consists of one House, before that House.

91. Amendment of Act 45 of 1860.—The Indian Penal Code shall be amended in the manner specified in the First Schedule to this Act.

92. Amendment of Act 1 of 1872.—The Indian Evidence Act, 1872 shall be amended in the manner specified in the Second Schedule to this Act.

93. Amendment of Act 18 of 1891.—The Bankers' Books Evidence Act, 1891 shall be amended in the manner specified in the Third Schedule to this Act.

94. Amendment of Act 2 of 1834.—The Reserve Bank of India Act, 1934 shall be amended in the manner specified in the Fourth Schedule to this Act.

The First Schedule

(See section 91)

Amendments to the Indian Penal Code
(45 of 1860)

1. After section 29, the following section shall be inserted, namely:—

"**29A.** *Electronic record.*—The words "electronic record" shall have the meaning assigned to them in clause (t) of sub-section (1) of section 2 of the Information Technology Act, 2000.".

2. In section 167, for the words "such public servant, charged with the preparation or translation of any document, frames or translates that document", the words "such public servant, charged with the preparation or translation of any document or electronic record, frames, prepares or translates that document or electronic record" shall be substituted.

3. In section 172, for the words "produce a document in a Court of Justice", the words "produce a document or an electronic record in a Court of Justice" shall be substituted.

4. In section 173, for the words "to produce a document in a Court of Justice", the words "to produce a document or electronic record in a Court of Justice" shall be substituted.

5. In section 175, for the word "document" at both the places where it occurs, the words "document or electronic record" shall be substituted.

6. In section 192, for the words "makes any false entry in any book or record, or makes any document containing a false statement", the words "makes any false entry in any book or record, or electronic record or makes any document or electronic record containing a false statement" shall be substituted.

7. In section 204, for the word "document" at both the places where it occurs, the words "document or electronic record" shall be substituted.

8. In section 463, for the words "Whoever makes any false documents or part of a document with intent to cause damage or injury", the words "Whoever makes any false documents or false electronic record or part of a document or electronic record, with intent to cause damage or injury" shall be substituted.

9. In section 464,—

(a) for the portion beginning with the words "A person is said to make a false document" and ending with the words "by reason of deception practised upon him, he does not know the contents of the document or the nature of the alteration", the following shall be substituted, namely:—

"A person is said to make a false document or false electronic record—

First—Who dishonestly or fraudulently—

(a) makes, signs, seals or executes a document or part of a document;

(b) makes or transmits any electronic record or part of any electronic record;

(c) affixes any digital signature on any electronic record;

(d) makes any mark denoting the execution of a document or the authenticity of the digital signature,

with the intention of causing it to be believed that such document or part of document, electronic record or digital signature was made, signed, sealed, executed, transmitted or affixed by or by the authority of a person by whom or by whose authority he knows that it was not made, signed, sealed, executed or affixed; or

Secondly—Who, without lawful authority, dishonestly or fraudulently, by cancellation or otherwise, alters a document or an electronic record in any material part thereof, after it has been made, executed or affixed with digital signature either by himself or by any other person, whether such person be living or dead at the time of such alteration; or

Thirdly—Who dishonestly or fraudulently causes any person to sign, seal, execute or alter a document or an electronic record or to affix his digital signature on any electronic record knowing that such person by reason of unsoundness of mind or intoxication cannot, or that by reason of deception practised upon him, he does not know the contents of the document or electronic record or the nature of the alteration. " ;

(b) after *Explanation* 2, the following *Explanation* shall be inserted at the end, namely:—

'*Explanation 3.*—For the purposes of this section, the expression "affixing digital signature" shall have the meaning assigned to it in clause (d) of sub-section (1) of section 2 of the Information Technology Act, 2000.'.

10. In section 466,—

(a) for the words "Whoever forges a document", the words "Whoever forges a document or an electronic record" shall be substituted;

(b) the following *Explanation* shall be inserted at the end, namely:—

'*Explanation.*—For the purposes of this section, "register" includes any list, data or record of any entries maintained in the electronic form as defined in clause *(r)* of sub-section (1) of section 2 of the Information Technology Act, 2000.'.

11. In section 468, for the words "document forged", the words "document or electronic record forged" shall be substituted.

12. In section 469, for the words "intending that the document forged", the words "intending that the document or electronic record forged" shall be substituted.

13. In section 470, for the word "document" in both the places where it occurs, the words "document or electronic record" shall be substituted.

14. In section 471, for the word "document" wherever it occurs, the words "document or electronic record" shall be substituted.

15. In section 474, for the portion beginning with the words "Whoever has in his possession any document" and ending with

the words "if the document is one of the description mentioned in section 466 of this Code", the following shall be substituted, namely: —

> "Whoever has in his possession any document or electronic record, knowing the same to be forged and intending that the same shall fraudulently or dishonestly be used as a genuine, shall, if the document or electronic record is one of the description mentioned in section 466 of this Code.".

16. In section 476, for the words "any document", the words "any document or electronic record" shall be substituted.

17. In section 477A, for the words "book, paper, writing" at both the places where they occur, the words "book, electronic record, paper, writing" shall be substituted.

The Second Schedule

(See section 92)

Amendments to the Indian Evidence Act, 1872

(1 of 1872)

1. In section 3,—

   (a) in the definition of "Evidence", for the words "all documents produced for the inspection of the Court", the words "all documents including electronic records produced for the inspection of the Court" shall be substituted;

   (b) after the definition of "India", the following shall be inserted, namely:—

   'the expressions "Certifying Authority", "digital signature", "Digital Signature Certificate","electronic form", "electronic records", "information", "secure electronic record", "secure digital signature" and "subscriber" shall have the meanings respectively assigned to them in the Information Technology Act, 2000.'.

2. In section 17, for the words "oral or documentary,", the words "oral or documentary or contained in electronic form" shall be substituted.

3. After section 22, the following section shall be inserted, namely: —

"**22A.** *When oral admission as to contents of electronic records are relevant.*—Oral admissions as to the contents of electronic records are not relevant, unless the genuineness of the electronic record produced is in question.".

4. In section 34, for the words "Entries in the books of account", the words "Entries in the books of account, including those maintained in an electronic form" shall be substituted.

5. In section 35, for the word "record", in both the places where it occurs, the words "record or an electronic record" shall be substituted.

6. For section 39, the following section shall be substituted, namely: —

"**39.** What evidence to be given when statement forms part of a conversation, document, electronic record, book or series of letters or papers. "39. When any statement of which evidence is given forms part of a longer statement, or of a conversation or pan of an isolated document, or is contained in a document which forms part of a book, or is contained in part of electronic record or of a connected series of letters or papers, evidence shall be given of so much and no more of the statement, conversation, document, electronic record, book or series of letters or papers as the Court considers necessary in that particular case to the full understanding of the nature and effect of the statement, and of the circumstances under which it was made.".

7. After section 47, the following section shall be inserted, namely: —

"**47A.** Opinion as to digital signature where relevant.—When the Court has to form an opinion as to the digital signature of any person, the opinion of the Certifying Authority which has issued the Digital Signature Certificate is a relevant fact.".

8. In section 59, for the words "contents of documents" the words "contents of documents or electronic records" shall be substituted.

9. After section 65, the following sections shall be inserted, namely:–

'**65A.** Special provisions as to evidence relating to electronic record. The contents of electronic records may be proved in accordance with the provisions of section 65B.

65B. Admissibility of electronic records. (1) Notwithstanding anything contained in this Act, any information contained in an electronic record which is printed on a paper, stored, recorded or copied in optical or magnetic media produced by a computer (hereinafter referred to as the computer output) shall be deemed to be also a document, if the conditions mentioned in this section are satisfied in relation to the information and computer in question and shall be admissible in any proceedings, without further proof or production of the original, as evidence of any contents of the original or of any fact stated therein of which direct evidence would be admissible.

(2) The conditions referred to in sub-section (1) in respect of a computer output shall be the following, namely: —

(a) the computer output containing the information was produced by the computer during the period over which the computer was used regularly to store or process information for the purposes of any activities regularly carried on over that period by the person having lawful control over the use of the computer;

(b) during the said period, information of the kind contained in the electronic record or of the kind from which the information so contained is derived was regularly fed into the computer in the ordinary course of the said activities;

(c) throughout the material part of the said period, the computer was operating properly or, if not, then in respect of any period in which it was not operating properly or was out of operation during that part of the period, was not such as to affect the electronic record or the accuracy of its contents; and

(d) the information contained in the electronic record reproduces or is derived from such information fed into the computer in the ordinary course of the said activities.

(3) Where over any period, the function of storing or processing information for the purposes of any activities regularly carried on over that period as mentioned in clause (a) of sub-section (2) was regularly performed by computers, whether—

(a) by a combination of computers operating over that period; or

(b) by different computers operating in succession over that period; or

(c) by different combinations of computers operating in succession over that period; or

(d) in any other manner involving the successive operation over that period, in whatever order, of one or more computers and one or more combinations of computers,

all the computers used for that purpose during that period shall be treated for the purposes of this section as constituting a single computer; and references in this section to a computer shall be construed accordingly.

(4) In any proceedings where it is desired to give a statement in evidence by virtue of this section, a certificate doing any of the following things, that is to say—

(a) identifying the electronic record containing the statement and describing the manner in which it was produced;

(b) giving such particulars of any device involved in the production of that electronic record as may be appropriate for the purpose of showing that the electronic record was produced by a computer;

(c) dealing with any of the matters to which the conditions mentioned in sub-section (2) relate, and purporting to be signed by a person occupying a responsible official position in relation to the operation of the relevant device or the management of the relevant activities (whichever is appropriate) shall be evidence of any matter stated in the certificate; and for the purposes of this sub-section it shall be sufficient for a matter to be stated to the best of the knowledge and belief of the person stating it.

(5) For the purposes of this section, —

(a) information shall be taken to be supplied to a computer if it is supplied thereto in any appropriate form and whether it is so supplied directly or (with or without human intervention) by means of any appropriate equipment;

(b) whether in the course of activities carried on by any official, information is supplied with a view to its being stored or processed for the purposes of those activities by a computer operated otherwise than in the course of those activities, that information, if duly supplied to that computer, shall be taken to be supplied to it in the course of those activities;

(c) a computer output shall be taken to have been produced by a computer whether it was produced by it directly or (with or without human intervention) by means of any appropriate equipment.

Explanation.—For the purposes of this section any reference to information being derived from other information shall be a reference to its being derived therefrom by calculation, comparison or any other process.

10. After section 67, the following section shall be inserted, namely: —

"**67A.** Proof as to digital signature. Except in the case of a secure digital signature, if the digital-signature of any subscriber is alleged to have been affixed to an electronic record the fact that such digital signature is the digital signature of the subscriber must be proved.".

11. After section 73, the following section shall be inserted, namely: —

'73A. Proof as to verification of digital signature. In order to ascertain whether a digital signature is that of the person by whom it purports to have been affixed, the Court may direct—

(a) that person or the Controller or the Certifying Authority to produce the Digital Signature Certificate;

(b) any other person to apply the public key listed in the Digital Signature Certificate and verify the digital signature purported to have been affixed by that person.

Explanation.—For the purposes of this section, "Controller" means the Controller appointed under sub-section (1) of section 17 of the Information Technology Act, 2000'.

12. After section 81, the following section shall be inserted, namely: —

"81 A. Presumption as to Gazettes in electronic forms.—The Court shall presume the genuineness of every electronic record purporting to be the Official Gazette, or purporting to be electronic record directed by any law to be kept by any person, if such electronic record is kept substantially in the form required by law and is produced from proper custody."

13. After section 85, the following sections shall be inserted, namely: —

"85A. Presumption as to electronic aggrements. The Court shall presume that every electronic record purporting to be an agreement containing the digital signatures of the parties was so concluded by affixing the digital signature of the parties.

85B. Presumption as to electronic records and digital signatures.— (1) In any proceedings involving a secure electronic record, the Court shall presume unless contrary is proved, that the secure electronic record has not been altered since the specific point of time to which the secure status relates.

(2) In any proceedings, involving secure digital signature, the Court shall presume unless the contrary is proved that—

(a) the secure digital signature is affixed by subscriber with the intention of signing or approving the electronic record;

(b) except in the case of a secure electronic record or a secure digital signature, nothing in this section shall create any presumption relating to authenticity and integrity of the electronic record or any digital signature."

85C. Presumption as to Digital Signature Certificates. The Court shall presume, unless contrary is proved, that the information listed in a Digital Signature Certificate is correct, except for information specified as subscriber information which has not been verified, if the certificate was accepted by the subscriber.".

14. After section 88, the following section shall be inserted, namely: —

'88A. Presumption as to electronic messages.— The Court may presume that an electronic message forwarded by the originator through an electronic mail server to the addressee to whom the message purports to be addressed corresponds with the message as fed into his computer for transmission; but the Court shall not make any presumption as to the person by whom such message was sent.

Explanation.—For the purposes of this section, the expressions "addressee" and "originator" shall have the same meanings respectively assigned to them in clauses *(b)* and (za) of sub-section (1) of section 2 of the Information Technology Act, 2000.'.

15. After section 90, the following section shall be inserted, namely:—

"90A. Presumption as to electronic records five years old. Where any electronic record, purporting or proved to be five years old, is produced from any custody which the Court in the particular case considers proper, the Court may presume that the digital signature which purports to be the digital signature of any particular person was so affixed by him or any person authorised by him in this behalf.

Explanation.—Electronic records are said to be in proper custody if they are in the place in which, and under the care of the person with whom, they naturally be; but no custody is improper if it is proved to have had a legitimate origin, or the circumstances of the particular case are such as to render such an origin probable.

This *Explanation* applies also to section 81A.".

16. For section 131, the following section shall be substituted, namely:—

"**131.** *Production of documents or electronic records which another person, having possession, could refuse to produce.*—No one shall be compelled to produce documents in his possession or electronic records under his control, which any other person would be entitled to refuse to produce if they were in his possession or control, unless such last-mentioned person consents to their production.".

The Third Schedule

(See section 93)

Amendments to the Bankers' Books Evidence Act, 891 (18 OF 1891)

1. In section 2—

(a) for clause (3), the following clause shall be substituted, namely:—

'(3) "bankers' books" include ledgers, day-books, cash-books, account-books and all other books used in the ordinary business of a bank whether kept in the written form or as printouts of data stored in a floppy, disc, tape or any other form of electro-magnetic data storage device;"

(b) *for* clause (8), the following clause shall be substituted, namely:—

'(8) "certified copy" means when the books of a bank,—

(a) are maintained in written form, a copy of any entry in such books together with a certificate written at; the foot of such copy that it is a true copy of such entry, that such entry is contained in one of the ordinary books of the bank and was made in the usual and ordinary course of business and that such book is still in the custody of the bank, and where the copy was obtained by a mechanical or other process which in itself ensured the accuracy of the copy, a further certificate to that effect, but where the book from which such copy was prepared has been destroyed in the usual course of the bank's business after the date on which the copy had been so prepared, a further certificate to that effect, each such certificate being dated and subscribed by the principal accountant or manager of the bank with his name and official title; and

(b) consist of printouts of data stored in a floppy, disc, tape or any other electro-magnetic data storage device, a printout of such entry or a copy of such printout together with such statements certified in accordance with the provisions of section 2A.'

2. After section 2, the following section shall be inserted, namely:—

"**2A.** Conditions in the printout. A printout of entry or a copy of printout referred to in sub-section *(8) of* section 2 shall be accompanied by the following, namely: —

(a) a certificate to the effect that it is a printout of such entry or a copy of such printout by the principal accountant or branch manager; and

(b) a certificate by a person in-charge of computer system containing a brief description of the computer system and the particulars of—

(A) the safeguards adopted by the system to ensure that data is entered or any other operation performed only by authorised persons;

(B) the safeguards adopted to prevent and detect unauthorised change of data;

(C) the safeguards available to retrieve data that is lost due to systemic failure or any other reasons;

(D) the manner in which data is transferred from the system to removable media like floppies, discs, tapes or other electro-magnetic data storage devices;

(E) the mode of verification in order to ensure that data has been accurately transferred to such removable media;

(F) the mode of identification of such data storage devices;

(G) the arrangements for the storage and custody of such storage devices;

(H) the safeguards to prevent and detect any tampering with the system; and

(I) any other factor which will vouch for the integrity and accuracy of the system.

(c) a further certificate from the person in-charge of the computer system to the effect that to the best of his knowledge and belief, such computer system operated properly at the material time, he was provided with all the relevant data and the printout in question represents correctly, or is appropriately derived from, the relevant data.".

The Fourth Schedule

(See section 94)

Amendment to the Reserve Bank of India Act, 1934 (2 oF 1934)

In the Reserve Bank of IndiaAct, 1934, in section 58, in sub-section (2), after clause *(p),* the following clause shall be inserted, namely:—

"*(pp)* the regulation of fund transfer through electronic means between the banks or between the banks and other financial institutions referred to in clause (c) of section 45-1, including the laying down of the conditions subject to which banks and other financial institutions shall participate in such fund transfers, the manner of such fund transfers and the rights and obligations of the participants in such fund transfers;".

The Information Technology (Certifying Authorities) Rules, 2000[1]

In exercise of the powers conferred by section 87 of the Information Technology Act, 2000 (21 of 2000), the Central Government hereby makes the following rules regulating the application and other guidelines for Certifying Authorities, namely:-

1. Short title and commencement.—(1) These Rules may be called Information Technology (Certifying Authorities) Rules, 2000.

(2) They shall come into force on the date of their publication in the Official Gazette.

2. Definitions.—In these Rules, unless the context otherwise requires,–

(a) "Act" means the Information Technology Act, 2000 (21 of 2000);

(b) "applicant" means Certifying Authority applicant;

---

1. Vide G.S.R. 789 (E), dated 17th October, 2000.

(c) "auditor" means any internationally accredited computer security professional or agency appointed by the Certifying Authority and recognized by the controller for conducting technical audit of operation of Certifying Authority;

(d) "Controller" means controller of Certifying Authority appointed under sub-section (1) of section 17 of the Act.

(e) "Digital Signature Certificate" means Digital Signature Certificate issued under sub-section (4) of section 35 of the Act;

(f) "information asset" means all information resources utilized in the course of any organisation's business and includes all information, applications (software developed or purchased), and technology (hardware, system software and networks);

(g) "licence" means a licence granted to Certifying Authorities for the issue of Digital Signature Certificates under these rules;

(h) "licensed Certifying Authority" means Certifying Authority who has been granted a licence to issue Digital Signature Certificates;

(i) "person" shall include an individual; or a company or association or body of individuals; whether incorporated or not; or Central Government or a State Government or any of the Ministries or Departments, Agencies or Authorities of such Governments;

(j) "Schedule" means a schedule annexed to these rules;

(k) "subscriber identity verification method" means the method used to verify and authenticate the identity of a subscriber;

(l) "trusted person" means any person who has:—

(i) direct responsibilities for the day-to-day operations, security and performance of those business activities that are regulated under the Act or these Rules in respect of a Certifying Authority; or

(ii) duties directly involving the issuance, renewal, suspension, revocation of Digital Signature Certificates (including the identification of any person requesting a Digital Signature Certificate from a licensed Certifying Authority), creation of private keys or administration of a Certifying Authority's computing facilities.

(m) words and expressions used herein and not defined but defined in Schedule-IV shall have the meaning respectively assigned to them in that schedule.

3. The manner in which information be authenticated by means of Digital Signature.—A Digital Signature shall,—

(a) be created and verified by cryptography that concerns itself with transforming electronic record into seemingly unintelligible forms and back again;

(b) use what is known as "Public Key Cryptography", which employs an algorithm using two different but mathematical related "keys" – one for creating a Digital Signature or transforming data into a seemingly unintelligible form, and another key for verifying a Digital Signature or returning the electronic record to original form,

the process termed as hash function shall be used in both creating and verifying a Digital Signature.

Explanation: Computer equipment and software utilizing two such keys are often termed as "asymmetric cryptography".

4. Creation of Digital Signature.—To sign an electronic record or any other item of information, the signer shall first apply the hash function in the signer's software; the hash function shall compute a hash result of standard length which is unique (for all practical purposes) to the electronic record; the signer's software transforming the hash result into a Digital Signature using signer's private key; the resulting Digital Signature shall be unique to both electronic record and private key used to create it; and the Digital Signature shall be attached to its electronic record and stored or transmitted with its electronic record.

5. Verification of Digital Signature.—The verification of a Digital Signature shall be accomplished by computing a new hash result of the original electronic record by means of the hash function used to create a Digital Signature and by using the public key and the new hash result, the verifier shall check–

(i) if the Digital Signature was created using the corresponding private key; and

(ii) if the newly computed hash result matches the original result which was transformed into Digital Signature during the signing process. The verification software will confirm the Digital Signature as verified if:–

(a) the signer's private key was used to digitally sign the electronic record, which is known to be the case if the signer's public key was used to verify the signature because the signer's public key will verify only a Digital Signature created with the signer's private key; and

(b) the electronic record was unaltered, which is known to be the case if the hash result computed by the verifier is identical to the hash result extracted from the Digital Signature during the verification process.

6. Standards.-The Information Technology (IT) architecture for Certifying Authorities may support open standards and accepted de facto standards; the most important standards that may be considered for different activities associated with the Certifying Authority's functions are as under:

The Product	The Standard
Public Key Infrastructure	PKIX
Digital Signature Certificates and Digital Signature revocation list	X.509. version 3 certificates as specified in ITU RFC 1422
Directory (DAP and LDAP)	X500 for publication of certificates and Certification Revocation Lists (CRLs)
Database Management Operations	Use of generic SQL
Public Key algorithm	DSA and RSA
Digital Hash Function	MD5 and SHA-1
RSA Public Key Technology	PKCS#1 RSA Encryption Standard (512, 1024, 2048 bit)
	PKCS#5 Password Based Encryption Standard
	PKCS#7 Cryptographic Message Syntax standard
	PKCS#8 Private Key Information Syntax standard
	PKCS#9 Selected Attribute Types
	PKCS#10 RSA Certification Request
	PKCS#12 Portable format for storing/transporting a user's private keys and certificates
Distinguished name	X.520
Digital Encryption and Digital Signature	PKCS#7
Digital Signature Request Format	PKCS#10

7. Digital Signature Certificate Standard.—All Digital Signature Certificates issued by the Certifying Authorities shall conform *to ITU X.509 version 3 standard* as per rule 6 and shall *inter alia* contain the following data, namely:-

(a) Serial Number (assigning of serial number to the Digital Signature Certificate by Certifying Authority to distinguish it from other certificate);

(b) Signature Algorithm Identifier (which identifies the algorithm used by Certifying Authority to sign the Digital Signature Certificate);

(c) Issuer Name (name of the Certifying Authority who issued the Digital Signature Certificate);

(d) Validity period of the Digital Signature Certificate;

(e) Name of the subscriber (whose public key the Certificate identifies); and

(f) Public Key information of the subscriber.

8. Licensing of Certifying Authorities.—(1) The following persons may apply for grant of a licence to issue Digital Signature Certificates, namely :-

(a) an individual, being a citizen of India and having a capital of five crores of rupees or more in his business or profession;

(b) a company having –

(i) paid up capital of not less than five crores of rupees; and

(ii) net worth of not less than fifty crores of rupees:

Provided that no company in which the equity share capital held in aggregate by the Non-resident Indians, Foreign Institutional Investors, or foreign companies, exceeds forty-nine per cent of its capital, shall be eligible for grant of licence:

Provided further that in a case where the company has been registered under the Companies Act, 1956 (1 of 1956) during the preceding financial year or in the financial year during which it applies for grant of licence under the Act and whose main object is to act as Certifying Authority, the net worth referred to in sub-clause (ii) of this clause shall be the aggregate net worth of its majority shareholders holding at least 51% of paid equity capital, being the Hindu Undivided Family, firm or company:

Provided also that the majority shareholders referred to in the second proviso shall not include Non-resident Indian, foreign national, Foreign Institutional Investor and foreign company:

Provided also that the majority shareholders of a company referred to in the second proviso whose net worth has been determined on the basis of such majority shareholders, shall not sell or transfer its equity shares held in such company-

(i) unless such a company acquires or has its own net worth of not less than fifty crores of rupees;

(ii) without prior approval of the Controller;

(c) a firm having –

(i) capital subscribed by all partners of not less than five crores of rupees; and

(ii) net worth of not less than fifty crores of rupees:

Provided that no firm, in which the capital held in aggregate by any Non-resident Indian, and foreign national, exceeds forty-nine per cent of its capital, shall be eligible for grant of licence:

Provided further that in a case where the firm has been registered under the Indian Partnership Act, 1932 (9 of 1932) during the preceding financial year or in the financial year during which it applies for grant of licence under the Act and whose main object is to act as Certifying Authority, the net worth referred to in sub-clause (ii) of this clause shall be the aggregate net worth of all of its partners:

Provided also that the partners referred to in the second proviso shall not include Non-resident Indian and foreign national:

Provided also that the partners of a firm referred to in the second proviso whose net worth has been determined on the basis of such partners, shall not sell or transfer its capital held in such firm-

(i) unless such firm has acquired or has its own net worth of not less than fifty crores of rupees;

(ii) without prior approval of the Controller;

(d) Central Government or a State Government or any of the Ministries or Departments, Agencies or Authorities of such Governments.

Explanation.-For the purpose of this rule,-

(i) "company" shall have the meaning assigned to it in clause 17 of section 2 of the Income-tax Act,1961 (43 of 1961);

(ii) "firm", "partner" and "partnership" shall have the meanings respectively assigned to them in the Indian Partnership Act, 1932 (9 of 1932); but the expression "partner" shall also include any person who, being a minor has been admitted to the benefits of partnership;

(iii) "foreign company" shall have the meaning assigned to it in clause (23A) of section 2 of the Income-tax Act,1961 (43 of 1961);

(iv) "net worth" shall have the meaning assigned to it in clause (ga) of sub-section (1) of section 3 of the Sick Industrial Companies (Special Provisions) Act, 1985 (1 of 1986);

(v) "Non-resident" shall have the meaning assigned to it as in clause 26 of section 2 of the Income-tax Act,1961 (43 of 1961).

(2) The applicant being an individual, or a company, or a firm under sub-rule (1), shall submit a performance bond or furnish a banker's guarantee from a scheduled bank in favour of the Controller in such form and in such manner as may be approved by the Controller for an amount of not less than five crores of rupees and the performance bond or banker's guarantee shall remain valid for a period of six years from the date of its submission:

Provided that the company and firm referred to in the second proviso to clause (b) and the second proviso to clause (c) of sub-rule (1) shall submit a performance bond or furnish a banker's guarantee for ten crores of rupees:

Provided further that nothing in the first proviso shall apply to the company or firm after it has acquired or has its net worth of fifty crores of rupees.

(3) Without prejudice to any penalty which may be imposed or prosecution may be initiated for any offence under the Act or any other law for the time being in force, the performance bond or banker's guarantee may be invoked—

(a) when the Controller has suspended the licence under sub-section (2) of section 25 of the Act; or

(b) for payment of an offer of compensation made by the Controller; or

(c) for payment of liabilities and rectification costs attributed to the negligence of the Certifying Authority, its officers or employees; or

(d) for payment of the costs incurred in the discontinuation or transfer of operations of the licensed Certifying Authority, if the Certifying Authority's licence or operations is discontinued; or

(e) any other default made by the Certifying Authority in complying with the provisions of the Act or rules made thereunder.

Explanation.—"transfer of operation" shall have the meaning assigned to it in clause (47) of section 2 of the Income-tax Act, 1961 (43 of 1961).

9. Location of the Facilities.—The infrastructure associated with all functions of generation, issue and management of Digital Signature Certificate as well as maintenance of Directories containing information about the status, and validity of Digital Signature Certificate shall be installed at any location in India.

10. Submission of Application.—Every application for a licensed Certifying Authority shall be made to the Controller,-

(i) in the form given at Schedule I; and

(ii) in such manner as the Controller may, from time to time, determine, supported by such documents and information as the Controller may require and it shall *inter alia* include—

(a) a Certification Practice Statement (CPS);

(b) a statement including the procedures with respect to identification of the applicant;

(c) a statement for the purpose and scope of anticipated Digital Signature Certificate technology, management, or operations to be outsourced;

(d) certified copies of the business registration documents of Certifying Authority that intends to be licensed;

(e) a description of any event, particularly current or past insolvency, that could materially affect the applicant's ability to act as a Certifying Authority;

(f) an undertaking by the applicant that to its best knowledge and belief it can and will comply with the requirements of its Certification Practice Statement;

(g) an undertaking that the Certifying Authority's operation would not commence until its operation and facilities associated with the functions of generation, issue and management of Digital Signature Certificate are audited by the auditors and approved by the Controller in accordance with rule 20;

(h) an undertaking to submit a performance bond or banker's guarantee in accordance with sub-rule (2) of rule 8 within one month of Controller indicating his approval for the grant of licence to operate as a Certifying Authority;

(i) any other information required by the Controller.

11. Fee.—(1) The application for the grant of a licence shall be accompanied by a non-refundable fee of twenty-five thousand rupees payable by a bank draft or by a pay order drawn in the name of the Controller.

(2) The application submitted to the Controller for renewal of Certifying Authority's licence shall be accompanied by a non-refundable fee of five thousand rupees payable by a bank draft or by a pay order drawn in the name of the Controller.

(3) Fee or any part thereof shall not be refunded if the licence is suspended or revoked during its validity period.

12. Cross Certification.—(1) The licensed Certifying Authority shall have arrangement for cross certification with other licensed Certifying Authorities within India which shall be submitted to the Controller before the commencement of their operations as per rule 20:

Provided that any dispute arising as a result of any such arrangement between the Certifying Authorities; or between Certifying Authorities or Certifying Authority and the Subscriber, shall be referred to the Controller for arbitration or resolution.

(2) The arrangement for Cross Certification by the licensed Certifying Authority with a Foreign Certifying Authority along with the application, shall be submitted to the Controller in such form and in such manner as may be provided in the regulations made by the Controller; and the licensed Certifying Authority shall not commence cross certification operations unless it has obtained the written or digital signature approval from the Controller.

13. Validity of licence.—(1) A licence shall be valid for a period of five years from the date of its issue.

(2) The licence shall not be transferable.

14. Suspension of Licence.—(1) The Controller may by order suspend the licence in accordance with the provisions contained in sub-section (2) of section 25 of the Act.

(2) The licence granted to the persons referred to in clauses (a) to (c) of sub-rule (1) of rule 8 shall stand suspended when the performance bond submitted or the banker's guarantee furnished by such persons is invoked under sub-rule (2) of that rule.

15. Renewal of licence.—(1) The provisions of rule 8 to rule 13, shall apply in the case of an application for renewal of a licence as it applies to a fresh application for licensed Certifying Authority.

(2) A Certifying Authority shall submit an application for the renewal of its licence not less than forty-five days before the date of expiry of the period of validity of licence.

(3) The application for renewal of licence may be submitted in the form of electronic record subject to such requirements as the Controller may deem fit.

16. Issuance of Licence.—(1) The Controller may, within four weeks from the date of receipt of the application, after considering the documents accompanying the application and such other factors, as he may deem fit, grant or renew the licence or reject the application:

Provided that in exceptional circumstances and for reasons to be recorded in writing, the period of four weeks may be extended to such period, not exceeding eight weeks in all as the Controller may deem fit.

(2) If the application for licensed Certifying Authority is approved, the applicant shall-

(a) submit a performance bond or furnish a banker's guarantee within one month from the date of such approval to the Controller in accordance with sub-rule (2) of rule 8; and

(b) execute an agreement with the Controller binding himself to comply with the terms and conditions of the licence and the provisions of the Act and the rules made thereunder.

17. Refusal of Licence.-The Controller may refuse to grant or renew a licence if—

(i) the applicant has not provided the Controller with such information relating to its business, and to any circumstances likely to affect its method of conducting business, as the Controller may require; or

(ii) the applicant is in the course of being wound up or liquidated; or

(iii) a receiver has, or a receiver and manager have, been appointed by the court in respect of the applicant; or

(iv) the applicant or any trusted person has been convicted, whether in India or out of India, of an offence the conviction for which involved a finding that it or such trusted person acted fraudulently or dishonestly, or has been convicted of an offence under the Act or these rules; or

(v) the Controller has invoked performance bond or banker's guarantee; or

(vi) a Certifying Authority commits breach of, or fails to observe and comply with, the procedures and practices as per the Certification Practice Statement; or

(vii) a Certifying Authority fails to conduct, or does not submit, the returns of the audit in accordance with rule 31; or

(viii) the audit report recommends that the Certifying Authority is not worthy of continuing Certifying Authority's operation; or

(ix) a Certifying Authority fails to comply with the directions of the Controller.

18. Governing Laws.—The Certification Practice Statement of the Certifying Authority shall comply with, and be governed by, the laws of the country.

19. Security Guidelines for Certifying Authorities.—(1) The Certifying Authorities shall have the sole responsibility of integrity, confidentiality and protection of information and information assets employed in its operation, considering classification, declassification, labeling, storage, access and destruction of information assets according to their value, sensitivity and importance of operation.

(2) Information Technology Security Guidelines and Security Guidelines for Certifying Authorities aimed at protecting the integrity, confidentiality and availability of service of Certifying Authority are given in Schedule-II and Schedule-III respectively.

(i) The Certifying Authority shall formulate its Information Technology and Security Policy for operation complying with these guidelines and submit it to the Controller before commencement of operation:

(ii) Provided that any change made by the Certifying Authority in the Information Technology and Security Policy shall be submitted by it within two weeks to the Controller.

20. Commencement of Operation by Licensed Certifying Authorities.—The licensed Certifying Authority shall commence its commercial operation of generation and issue of Digital Signature only after-

(a) it has confirmed to the Controller the adoption of Certification Practice Statement;

(b) it has generated its key pair, namely, private and corresponding public key, and submitted the public key to the Controller;

(c) the installed facilities and infrastructure associated with all functions of generation, issue and management of Digital Signature Certificate have been audited by the accredited auditor in accordance with the provisions of rule 31; and

(d) it has submitted the arrangement for cross certification with other licensed Certifying Authorities within India to the Controller.

21. Requirements Prior to Cessation as Certifying Authority.—Before ceasing to act as a Certifying Authority, a Certifying Authority shall,—

(a) give notice to the Controller of its intention to cease acting as a Certifying Authority:

Provided that the notice shall be made ninety days before ceasing to act as a Certifying Authority or ninety days before the date of expiry of licence;

(b) advertise sixty days before the expiry of licence or ceasing to act as Certifying Authority, as the case may be, the intention in such daily newspaper or newspapers and in such manner as the Controller may determine;

(c) notify its intention to cease acting as a Certifying Authority to the subscriber and Cross Certifying Authority of each unrevoked or unexpired Digital Signature Certificate issued by it :

Provided that the notice shall be given sixty days before ceasing to act as a Certifying Authority or sixty days before the date of expiry of unrevoked or unexpired Digital Signature Certificate, as the case may be;

(d) the notice shall be sent to the Controller, affected subscribers and Cross Certifying Authorities by digitally signed e-mail and registered post;

(e) revoke all Digital Signature Certificates that remain unrevoked or unexpired at the end of the ninety days notice period, whether or not the subscribers have requested revocation;

(f) make a reasonable effort to ensure that discontinuing its certification services causes minimal disruption to its subscribers and to persons duly needing to verify digital signatures by reference to the public keys contained in outstanding Digital Signature Certificates;

(g) make reasonable arrangements for preserving the records for a period of seven years;

(h) pay reasonable restitution (not exceeding the cost involved in obtaining the new Digital Signature Certificate) to subscribers for revoking the Digital Signature Certificates before the date of expiry;

(i) after the date of expiry mentioned in the licence, the Certifying Authority shall destroy the certificate–signing private key and confirm the date and time of destruction of the private key to the Controller.

22. Database of Certifying Authorities.—The Controller shall maintain a database of the disclosure record of every Certifying Authority, Cross Certifying Authority and Foreign Certifying Authority, containing *inter alia* the following details:

(a) the name of the person/names of the Directors, nature of business, Income-tax Permanent Account Number, web address, if any, office and residential address, location of facilities associated with functions of generation of Digital Signature Certificate, voice and facsimile telephone numbers, electronic mail address(es), administrative contacts and authorized representatives;

(b) the public key(s), corresponding to the private key(s) used by the Certifying Authority and recognized foreign Certifying Authority to digitally sign Digital Signature Certificate;

(c) current and past versions of Certification Practice Statement of Certifying Authority;

(d) time stamps indicating the date and time of-

(i) grant of licence;

(ii) confirmation of adoption of Certification Practice Statement and its earlier versions by Certifying Authority;

(iii) commencement of commercial operations of generation and issue of Digital Signature Certificate by the Certifying Authority;

(iv) revocation or suspension of licence of Certifying Authority;

(v) commencement of operation of Cross Certifying Authority;

(vi) issue of recognition of foreign Certifying Authority;

(vii) revocation or suspension of recognition of foreign Certifying Authority.

23. Digital Signature Certificate.—The Certifying Authority shall, for issuing the Digital Signature Certificates, while complying with the provisions of section 35 of the Act, also comply with the following, namely:-

(a) the Digital Signature Certificate shall be issued only after a Digital Signature Certificate application in the form provided by the Certifying Authority has been submitted by the subscriber to the Certifying Authority and the same has been approved by it:

Provided that the application Form contains, *inter alia*, the particulars given in the modal Form given in Schedule-IV;

(b) no interim Digital Signature Certificate shall be issued;

(c) the Digital Signature Certificate shall be generated by the Certifying Authority upon receipt of an authorised and validated request for:-

(i) new Digital Signature Certificates;

(ii) Digital Signature Certificates renewal;

(d) the Digital Signature Certificate must contain or incorporate, by reference such information, as is sufficient to locate or identify one or more repositories in which revocation or suspension of the Digital Signature Certificate will be listed, if the Digital Signature Certificate is suspended or revoked;

(e) the subscriber identity verification method employed for issuance of Digital Signature Certificate shall be specified in the Certification Practice Statement and shall be subject to the approval of the Controller during the application for a licence;

(f) where the Digital Signature Certificate is issued to a person (referred to in this clause as a New Digital Signature Certificate) on the basis of another valid Digital Signature Certificate held by the said person (referred in this clause as an Originating Digital Signature Certificate) and subsequently the originating Digital Signature Certificate has been suspended or revoked, the Certifying Authority that issued the new Digital Signature Certificate shall conduct investigations to determine whether it is necessary to suspend or revoke the new Digital Signature Certificate;

(g) the Certifying Authority shall provide a reasonable opportunity for the subscriber to verify the contents of the Digital Signature Certificate before it is accepted;

(h) if the subscriber accepts the issued Digital Signature Certificate, the Certifying Authority shall publish a signed copy of the Digital Signature Certificate in a repository;

(i) where the Digital Signature Certificate has been issued by the licensed Certifying Authority and accepted by the subscriber, and the Certifying Authority comes to know of any fact, or otherwise, that affects the validity or reliability of such Digital Signature Certificate, it shall notify the same to the subscriber immediately;

(j) all Digital Signature Certificates shall be issued with a designated expiry date.

24. Generation of Digital Signature Certificate.—The generation of the Digital Signature Certificate shall involve:

(a) receipt of an approved and verified Digital Signature Certificate request;

(b) creating a new Digital Signature Certificate;

(c) binding the key pair associated with the Digital Signature Certificate to a Digital Signature Certificate owner;

(d) issuing the Digital Signature Certificate and the associated public key for operational use;

(e) a distinguished name associated with the Digital Signature Certificate owner; and

(f) a recognized and relevant policy as defined in Certification Practice Statement.

25. Issue of Digital Signature Certificate. Before the issue of the Digital Signature Certificate, the Certifying Authority shall:-

(i) confirm that the user's name does not appear in its list of compromised users;

(ii) comply with the procedure as defined in his Certification Practice Statement including verification of identification and/or employment;

(iii) comply with all privacy requirements;

(iv) obtain a consent of the person requesting the Digital Signature Certificate, that the details of such Digital Signature Certificate can be published on a directory service.

26. Certificate Lifetime.—(1) A Digital Signature Certificate,-

(a) shall be issued with a designated expiry date;

(b) which is suspended shall return to the operational use, if the suspension is withdrawn in accordance with the provisions of section 37 of the Act;

(c) shall expire automatically upon reaching the designated expiry date at which time the Digital Signature Certificate shall be archived;

(d) on expiry, shall not be re-used.

(2) The period for which a Digital Signature Certificate has been issued shall not be extended, but a new Digital Signature Certificate may be issued after the expiry of such period.

27. Archival of Digital Signature Certificate.—A Certifying Authority shall archive—

(a) applications for issue of Digital Signature Certificates;

(b) registration and verification documents of generated Digital Signature Certificates;

(c) Digital Signature Certificates;

(d) notices of suspension;

(e) information of suspended Digital Signature Certificates;

(f) information of revoked Digital Signature Certificates;

(g) expired Digital Signature Certificates,

for a minimum period of seven years or for a period in accordance with legal requirement.

28. Compromise of Digital Signature Certificate.—Digital Signature Certificates in operational use that become compromised shall be revoked in accordance with the procedure defined in the Certification Practice Statement of Certifying Authority.

Explanation : Digital Signature Certificates shall,-

(a) be deemed to be compromised where the integrity of:—

  (i) the private key associated with the Digital Signature Certificate is in doubt;

  (ii) the Digital Signature Certificate owner is in doubt, as to the use, or attempted use of his key pairs, or otherwise, for malicious or unlawful purposes;

(b) remain in the compromised state for only such time as it takes to arrange for revocation.

29. Revocation of Digital Signature Certificate.—(1) Digital Signature Certificate shall be revoked and become invalid for any trusted use, where—

(a) there is a compromise of the Digital Signature Certificate owner's private key;

(b) there is a misuse of the Digital Signature Certificate;

(c) there is a misrepresentation or errors in the Digital Signature Certificate;

(d) the Digital Signature Certificate is no longer required.

(2) The revoked Digital Signature Certificate shall be added to the Certificate Revocation List (CRL).

30. Fees for issue of Digital Signature Certificate.—(1) The Certifying Authority shall charge such fee for the issue of Digital Signature Certificate as may be prescribed by the Central Government under sub-section (2) of section 35 of the Act.

(2) Fee may be payable in respect of access to Certifying Authority's X.500 directory for certificate downloading. Where fees are payable, Certifying Authority shall provide an up-to-date fee schedule to all its subscribers and users, this may be done by publishing fee schedule on a nominated website.

(3) Fees may be payable in respect of access to Certifying Authority's X.500 directory service for certificate revocation or status information. Where fees are payable, Certifying Authority shall provide an up-to-date fee schedule to all its subscribers and users, this may be done by publishing the fee schedule on a nominated website.

(4) No fee is to be levied for access to Certification Practice Statement via Internet. A fee may be charged by the Certifying Authority for providing printed copies of its Certification Practice Statement.

31. Audit.—(1) The Certifying Authority shall get its operations audited annually by an auditor and such audit shall include *inter alia*,-

(i) security policy and planning;
(ii) physical security;
(iii) technology evaluation;
(iv) Certifying Authority's services administration;
(v) relevant Certification Practice Statement;
(vi) compliance to relevant Certification Practice Statement;
(vii) contracts/agreements;
(viii) regulations prescribed by the Controller;
(ix) policy requirements of Certifying Authorities Rules, 2000.

(2) The Certifying Authority shall conduct,-

(a) half yearly audit of the security policy, physical security and planning of its operation;
(b) a quarterly audit of its repository.

(3) The Certifying Authority shall submit copy of each audit report to the Controller within four weeks of the completion of such audit and where irregularities are found, the Certifying Authority shall take immediate appropriate action to remove such irregularities.

32. Auditor's relationship with Certifying Authority.—(1) The auditor shall be independent of the Certifying Authority being audited and shall not be a software or hardware vendor which is, or has been providing services or supplying equipment to the said Certifying Authority.

(2) The auditor and the Certifying Authority shall not have any current or planned financial, legal or other relationship, other than that of an auditor and the audited party.

33. Confidential Information.—The following information shall be confidential namely:—

(a) Digital Signature Certificate application, whether approved or rejected;

(b) Digital Signature Certificate information collected from the subscriber or elsewhere as part of the registration and verification record but not included in the Digital Signature Certificate information;

(c) subscriber agreement.

34. Access to Confidential Information.—(1) Access to confidential information by Certifying Authority's operational staff shall be on a "need-to-know" and "need-to-use" basis.

(2) Paper based records, documentation and backup data containing all confidential information as prescribed in rule 33 shall be kept in secure and locked container or filing system, separately from all other records.

(3) The confidential information shall not be taken out of the country except in a case where a properly constitutional warrant or other legally enforceable document is produced to the Controller and he permits to do so.

Schedule-I

[See rule 10]

Form for Application for grant of Licence to be a Certifying Authority

For Individual

1. Full Name* _____ Last Name/Surname _____ First Name _____ Middle Name _____.

2. Have you ever been known by any other name? If Yes, Last Name/ Surname _____ First Name _____ Middle Name._____

3. Address

A. Residential Address * Flat/Door/Block No. _____ Name of Premises/ Building/Village _____ Road/Street/Lane/Post Office _____ Area/Locality/ Taluka/Sub-Division _____ Town/City/District.

State/Union Territory_____ Pin: _____ Telephone No _____ Fax _____ Mobile Phone No. _____

B. Office Address * Name of Office _____ Flat/Door/Block No. _____ Name of Premises/Building/Village _____ Road/Street/Lane/Post Office _____ Area/Locality/Taluka/Sub-Division _____ Town/City/District _____ State/ Union Territory _____ Pin _____ Telephone No. _____ Fax _____

4.Address for Communication * Tick [ ] as applicable A □ □or B □

5. Father's Name * Last Name/Surname _____ First Name _____ Middle Name _____

6. Sex * (For Individual Applicant only) Tick [ ] as applicable : Male / Female

7. Date of Birth (dd/mm/yyyy) * _____

8. Nationality * _____

9. Credit Card Details/Credit Card Type _____ Credit Card No. _____Issued By _____

10. E-mail Address _____

11. Web URL address _____

12. Passport Details # Passport No. _____ Passport issuing authority _____ Passport expiry date (dd/mm/yyyy) _____

13.Voter's Identity Card No. _____

14. Income Tax PAN no. _____

15. ISP Details ISP Name * _____ ISP's Website Address, if any _____Your User Name at ISP, if any _____

16. Personal Web page URL address, if any _____

17. Capital in the business or profession * Rs _____ (Attach documentary proof) For Company /Firm/Body of Individuals/Association of Persons/ Local Authority

18. Registration Number * ______

19. Date of Incorporation/Agreement/Partnership * ______

20:Particulars of Business, if any: * Head Office ____ Name of Office Flat/Door/Block No. ____ Name of Premises/Building/Village ____ Road/ Street/Lane/Post Office ____ Area/Locality/Taluka/Sub-Division ____ Town/ City/District ____ Pin ____ State/Union Territory ____ Telephone No. ____ Fax ____ Web page URL address, if any ____ of Branches ____ Nature of Business ______

21. Income Tax PAN No.* ______

22. Turnover in the last financial year Rs ______

23. Net worth * Rs ______

(Attach documentary proof)

24. Paid up Capital * Rs. ______

(Attach documentary proof)

25. Insurance Details Insurance Policy No.*____InsurerCompany * ______

26. Names, Addresses etc. of Partners/Members/Directors (For Information about more persons, please add separate sheet(s) in the format given in the next page) * No. of Partners/Members/Directors ______

Details of Partners/Members/Directors

A. Full Name ____ Last Name/Surname ____ First Name ____ Middle Name ____

B. Address Flat/Door/Block No. ____ Name of Premises/Building/ Village ____ Road/Street/Lane/Post Office ____ Area/Locality/ Taluka/Sub-Division ____ Town/City/District ____State/ Union Territory Pin ____ Telephone No. ____ Fax No. ____ Mobile Phone No. ______

C. Nationality ____ In case of foreign national, Visa details ____

D. Passport Details/Passport No. ____ Passport issuing authority ____ Passport expiry date ______

E. Voter's Identity Card No. ______

F. Income Tax PAN no. ______

G. E-mail Address ______

H. Personal Web page URL, if any ______

27. Authorised Representative * Name ____ Flat/Door/Block No. ____ Name of Premises/Building/Village ____ Road/Street/Lane/Post Office ____ Area/Locality/Taluka/Sub-Division ____ Town/City/District ____ Pin ____ State/Union Territory ____ Telephone No. ____ Fax ____ Nature of Business ______

For Government Ministry/Department/Agency/Authority

28. Particulars of Organisation: Name of Organisation _____ Administrative Ministry/Department _____ Under State/Central Government _____ Flat/Door/Block No. _____ Name of Premises/Building/Village _____ Road/Street/Lane/Post Office _____ Area/Locality/Taluka/Sub-Division _____ Town/City/District _____ Pin _____ State/Union Territory _____ Telephone No. _____ Fax No. _____ Web page URL Address _____ Name of the Head of Organisation _____ Designation _____ E-mail Address _____

29. Bank Details Bank Name _____ Branch _____ Bank Account No. _____ Type of Bank Account _____

30. Whether bank draft/pay order for licence fee enclosed * : Y / N

If yes, Name of Bank _____ Draft/pay order No. _____ Date of Issue Amount _____

31. Location of facility in India for generation of Digital Signature Certificate

32. Public Key _____

33. Whether undertaking for Bank Guarantee/Performance Bond attached * : Y / N

(Not applicable if the applicant is a Government Ministry/Department/ Agency/ Authority)

34. Whether Certification Practice Statement is enclosed * : Y / N

35. Whether certified copies of business registration document are enclosed:Y/N (For Company/ Firm/ Body of Individuals/ Association of Persons/ Local Authority) If yes, the documents attached:

ii) _____

iii) _____

iv) _____

36. Any other information _____

Date

Signature of the Applicant

_____

Instructions : 1. Columns marked with * are mandatory.

2. For the columns marked with #, details for at least one is mandatory.

3. Column No. 1 to 17 are to be filled up by individual applicant.

4. Column No. 18 to 27 are to be filled up if applicant is a Company/ Firm/ Body of Individuals/ Association of Persons/ Local Authority.

5. Column No. 28 is to be filled up if applicant is a Government organisation.

6. Column No., 29, 30, 31 and 34 are to be filled up by all applicants.

7. @Column No. 32 is applicable only for application for renewal of licence.

8. Column No. 33 is not applicable if the applicant is a Government organisation.

Schedule-II

[*See* rule 19(2)]

Information Technology (IT) Security Guidelines

1. Introduction—This document provides guidelines for the implementation and management of Information Technology Security. Due to the inherent dynamism of the security requirements, this document does not provide an exact template for the organizations to follow. However, appropriate suitable samples of security process are provided for guidelines. It is the responsibility of the organizations to develop internal processes that meet the guidelines set forth in this document.

The following words used in the Information Technology Security Guidelines shall be interpreted as follows:—

- shall: The guideline defined is a mandatory requirement, and therefore must be complied with.
- should: The guideline defined is a recommended requirement. Non-compliance shall be documented and approved by the management. Where appropriate, compensating controls shall be implemented.
- must: The guideline defined is a mandatory requirement, and therefore must be complied with.
- may: The guideline defined is an optional requirement. The implementation of this guideline is determined by the organisation's requirement.

2. Implementation of an Information Security Programme.—Successful implementation of a meaningful Information Security Programme rests with the support of the top management. Until and unless the senior managers of the organization understand and concur with the objectives of the information security programme its ultimate success is in question.

The Information Security Programme should be broken down into specific stages as follows:

(a) Adoption of a security policy;

(b) Security risk analysis;

(c) Development and implementation of a information classification system;

(d) Development and implementation of the security standards manual;

(e) Implementation of the management security self-assessment process;

(f) On-going security programme maintenance and enforcement; and

(g) Training.

The principal task of the security implementation is to define the responsibilities of persons within the organization. The implementation should be based on the general principle that the person who is generating the information is also responsible for its security. However, in order to enable him to carry out his responsibilities in this regard, proper tools, and environment need to be established.

When different pieces of information at one level are integrated to form higher value information, the responsibility for its security needs also should go up in the hierarchy to the integrator and should require higher level of authority for its access. It should be absolutely clear with respect to each information as to who is its owner, its custodian, and its users. It is the duty of the owner to assign the right classification to the information so that the required level of security can be enforced. The custodian of information is responsible for the proper implementation of security guidelines and making the information available to the users on a need to know basis.

3. Information Classification.—Information assets must be classified according to their sensitivity and their importance to the organization. Since it is unrealistic to expect managers and employees to maintain absolute control over all information within the boundaries of the organization, it is necessary to advise them on which types of information are considered more sensitive, and how the organization would like the sensitive information handled and protected. Classification, declassification, labeling, storage, access, destruction and reproduction of classified data and the administrative overhead this process will create must be considered. Failure to maintain a balance between the value of the information classified and the administrative burden the classification system places on the organization will result in long-term difficulties in achieving success.

Confidential is that classification of information of which unauthorized disclosure/use could cause serious damage to the organization, e.g. strategic planning documents.

Restricted is that classification of information of which unauthorized disclosure/use would not be in the best interest of the organization and/or its customers, e.g. design details, computer software (programs, utilities), documentation, organization personnel data, budget information.

Internal use is that classification of information that does not require any degree of protection against disclosure within the company, e.g. operating procedures, policies and standards inter office memorandums.

Unclassified is that classification of information that requires no protection against disclosure e.g. published annual reports, periodicals.

While the above classifications are appropriate for a general organization view point, the following classifications may be considered :

Top Secret: It shall be applied to information unauthorized disclosure of which could be expected to cause exceptionally grave damage to the national security or national interest. This category is reserved for Nation's closest secrets and to be used with great reserve.

Secret: This shall be applied to information unauthorized disclosure of which could be expected to cause serious damage to the national security or national interest or cause serious embarrassment in its functioning. This classification should be used for highly important information and is the highest classification normally used.

Confidentiality: This shall be applied to information unauthorized disclosure of which could be expected to cause damage to the security of the organisation or could be prejudicial to the interest of the organisation, or could affect the organisation in its functioning. Most information will on proper analysis be classified no higher than confidential.

Restricted: This shall be applied to information which is essentially meant for official use only and which would not be published or communicated to anyone except for official purpose.

Unclassified: This is the classification of information that requires no protection against disclosure.

4. Physical and Operational Security

***4.1 Site Design.*—(1)** The site shall not be in locations that are prone to natural or man-made disasters, like flood, fire, chemical contamination and explosions.

(2) As per nature of the operations, suitable floor structuring, lighting, power and water damage protection requirements shall be provided.

(3) Construction shall comply with all applicable building and safety regulations as laid down by the relevant Government agencies. Further, the construction must be tamper-evident.

(4) Materials used for the construction of the operational site shall be fire-resistant and free of toxic chemicals.

(5) External walls shall be constructed of brick or reinforced concrete of sufficient thickness to resist forcible attack. Ground level windows shall be fortified with sturdy mild steel grills or impact-resistant laminated security glass. All internal walls must be from the floor to the ceiling and must be tamper-evident.

(6) Air-conditioning system, power supply system and uninterrupted power supply unit with proper backup shall be installed depending upon the nature of operation. All ducting

holes of the air-conditioning system must be designed so as to prevent intrusion of any kind.

(7) Automatic fire detection, fire suppression systems and equipment in compliance with requirement specified by the Fire Brigade or any other agencies of the Central or State Government shall be installed at the operational site.

(8) Media library, electrical and mechanical control rooms shall be housed in separate isolated areas, with access granted only to specific, named individuals on a need basis.

(9) Any facility that supports mission-critical and sensitive applications must be located and designed for repairability, relocation and reconfiguration. The ability to relocate, reconstitute and reconfigure these applications must be tested as part of the business continuity/ disaster recovery plan.

4.2 Fire Protection

(1) Combustible materials shall not be stored within hundred meters of the operational site.

(2) Automatic fire detection, fire suppression systems and audible alarms as prescribed by the Fire Brigade or any other agency of the Central or State Government shall be installed at the operational site.

(3) Fire extinguishers shall be installed at the operational site and their locations clearly marked with appropriate signs.

(4) Periodic testing, inspection and maintenance of the fire equipment and fire suppression systems shall be carried out.

(5) Procedures for the safe evacuation of personnel in an emergency shall be visibly pasted/displayed at prominent places at the operational site. Periodic training and fire drills shall be conducted.

(6) There shall be no eating, drinking or smoking in the operational site. The work areas shall be kept clean at all times.

4.3 Environmental Protection.—(1) Water detectors shall be installed under the raised floors throughout the operational site and shall be connected to audible alarms.

(2) The temperature and humidity condition in the operational site shall be monitored and controlled periodically.

(3) Personnel at the operational site shall be trained to monitor and control the various equipment and devices installed at the operational site for the purpose of fire and environment protection.

(4) Periodic inspection, testing and maintenance of the equipment and systems shall be scheduled.

4.4 Physical Access.—(1) Responsibilities round the clock, seven days a week, three hundred sixty five days a year for physical security of the systems used for operation and also actual physical layout at the site of operation shall be defined and assigned to named individuals.

(2) Biometric physical access security systems shall be installed to control and audit access to the operational site.

(3) Physical access to the operational site at all times shall be controlled and restricted to authorised personnel only. Personnel authorized for limited physical access shall not be allowed to gain unauthorized access to restricted area within operational site.

(4) Dual control over the inventory and issue of access cards/keys during normal business hours to the Data Centre shall be in place. An up-to-date list of personnel who possess the cards/keys shall be regularly maintained and archived for a period of three years.

(5) Loss of access cards/keys must be immediately reported to the security supervisor of the operational site who shall take appropriate action to prevent unauthorised access.

(6) All individuals, other than operations staff, shall sign in and sign out of the operational site and shall be accompanied by operations staff.

(7) Emergency exits shall be tested periodically to ensure that the access security systems are operational.

(8) All opening of the Data Centre should be monitored round the clock by surveillance video cameras.

5. Information Management

5.1 System Administration.—(1) Each organization shall designate a properly trained "System Administrator" who will ensure that the protective security measures of the system are functional and who will maintain its security posture. Depending upon the complexity and security needs of a system or application, the System Administrator may have a designated System Security Administrator who will assume security responsibilities and provide physical, logical and procedural safeguards for information.

(2) Organisations shall ensure that only a properly trained System Security Administrator is assigned the system security responsibilities.

(3) The responsibility to create, classify, retrieve, modify, delete or archive information must rest only with the System Administrator.

(4) Any password used for the system administration and operation of trusted services must not be written down (in paper or electronic form) or shared with any one. A system for password management should be put in place to cover the eventualities such as forgotten password or changeover to another person in case of System Administrator (or System Security Administrator) leaving the organization. Every instance of usage of administrator's passwords must be documented.

(5) Periodic review of the access rights of all users must be performed.

(6) The System Administrator must promptly disable access to a user's account if the user is identified as having left the Data Centre, changed assignments, or is no longer requiring system access. Reactivation of the user's account must be authorized in writing by the System Administrator (Digitally signed e-mail may be acceptable).

(7) The System Administrator must take steps to safeguards classified information as prescribed by its owner.

(8) The System Administrator must authorize privileged access to users only on a need-to-know and need-to-do basis and also only after the authorization is documented.

(9) Criteria for the review of audit trails/access logs, reporting of access violations and procedures to ensure timely management action/response shall be established and documented.

(10) All security violations must be recorded, investigated, and periodic status reports compiled for review by the management.

(11) The System Administrator together with the system support staff, shall conduct a regular analysis of problems reported to and identify any weaknesses in protection of the information.

(12) The System Administrator shall ensure that the data, file and Public Key Infrastructure (PKI) servers are not left unmonitored while these systems are powered on.

(13) The System Administrator should ensure that no generic user is enabled or active on the system.

5.2 Sensitive Information Control

(1) Information assets shall be classified and protected according to their sensitivity and criticality to the organization.

(2) Procedures in accordance with para 8.3 of these Guidelines must be in place to handle the storage media, which has sensitive and classified information.

(3) All sensitive information stored in any media shall bear or be assigned an appropriate security classification.

(4) All sensitive material shall be stamped or labeled accordingly.

(5) Storage media (i.e. floppy diskettes, magnetic tapes, portable hard disks, optical disks, etc.) containing sensitive information shall be secured according to their classification.

(6) Electronic communication systems, such as router, switches, network device and computers, used for transmission of sensitive information should be equipped or installed with suitable security software and if necessary with an encryptor or encryption software. The appropriate procedure in this regard should be documented.

(7) Procedures shall be in place to ensure the secure disposal of sensitive information assets on all corrupted/damaged or affected media both internal (e.g. hard disk/optical disk) and

external (e.g. diskette, disk drive, tapes etc.) to the system. Preferably such affected/corrupted/damaged media both internal and external to the system shall be destroyed.

5.3 Sensitive Information Security

(1) Highly sensitive information assets shall be stored on secure removable media and should be in an encrypted format to avoid compromise by unauthorized persons.

(2) Highly sensitive information shall be classified in accordance with para 3.

(3) Sensitive information and data, which are stored on the fixed disk of a computer shared by more than one person, must be protected by access control software (e.g., password). Security packages must be installed which partition or provide authorization to segregated directories/files.

(4) Removable electronic storage media must bc removed from the computer and properly secured at the end of the work session or workday.

(5) Removable electronic storage media containing sensitive information and data must be clearly labeled and secured.

(6) Hard disks containing sensitive information and data must be securely erased prior to giving the computer system to another internal or external department or for maintenance.

5.4 Third Party Access.—(1) Access to the computer systems by other organisations shall be subjected to a similar level of security protection and controls as in these Information Technology security guidelines.

(2) In case the Data Centre uses the facilities of external service/facility provider (outsourcer) for any of their operations, the use of external service/facility providers (e.g. outsourcer) shall be evaluated in light of the possible security exposures and risks involved and all such agreements shall be approved by the information asset owner. The external service or facility provider shall also sign non-disclosure agreements with the management of the Data Centre/operational site.

(3) The external service/facility provider (e.g. outsourcer) shall provide an equivalent level of security controls as required by these Information Technology Security Guidelines.

5.5 Prevention of Computer Misuse.—(1) Prevention, detection, and deterrence measures shall be implemented to safeguard the security of computers and computer information from misuse. The measures taken shall be properly documented and reviewed regularly.

(2) Each organization shall provide adequate information to all persons, including management, systems developers and programmers, end-users, and third party users warning them against misuse of computers.

(3) Effective measures to deal expeditiously with breaches of security shall be established within each organisation. Such measures shall include :

- (i) Prompt reporting of suspected breach;
- (ii) Proper investigation and assessment of the nature of suspected breach;
- (iii) Secure evidence and preserve integrity of such material as relates to the discovery of any breach;
- (iv) Remedial measures.

(4) All incidents related to breaches shall be reported to the System Administrator or System Security Administrator for appropriate action to prevent future occurrence.

(5) Procedure shall be set-up to establish the nature of any alleged abuse and determine the subsequent action required to be taken to prevent its future occurrence. Such procedures shall include:

- (i) The role of the System Administrator, System Security Administrator and management;
- (ii) Procedure for investigation;
- (iii) Areas for security review; and
- (iv) Subsequent follow-up action.

6. System integrity and security measures.

6.1 Use of Security Systems or Facilities.—(1) Security controls shall be installed and maintained on each computer system or computer node to prevent unauthorised users from gaining entry to the information system and to prevent unauthorised access to data.

(2) Any system software or resource of the computer system should only be accessible after being authenticated by access control system.

6.2 System Access Control.—(1) Access control software and system software security features shall be implemented to protect resources. Management approval is required to authorise issuance of user identification (ID) and resource privileges.

(2) Access to information system resources like memory, storage devices etc., sensitive utilities and data resources and programme files shall be controlled and restricted based on a "need-to-use" basis with proper segregation of duties.

(3) The access control software or operating system of the computer system shall provide features to restrict access to the system and data resources. The use of common passwords such as "administrator" or "president" or "game" etc. to protect access to the system and data resources represent a security exposure and shall be avoided. All passwords used must be resistant to dictionary attacks.

(4) Appropriate approval for the request to access system resources shall be obtained from the System Administrator. Guidelines and procedures governing access authorisations shall be developed, documented and implemented.

(5) An Access Control System manual documenting the access granted to different level of users shall be prepared to provide guidance to the System Administrator for grant of access.

(6) Each user shall be assigned a unique user ID. Adequate user education shall be provided to help users in password choice and password protection. Sharing of user IDs shall not be allowed.

(7) Stored passwords shall be encrypted using internationally proven encryption techniques to prevent unauthorised disclosure and modification.

(8) Stored passwords shall be protected by access controls from unauthorised disclosure and modification.

(9) Automatic time-out for terminal inactivity should be implemented.

(10) Audit trail of security-sensitive access and actions taken shall be logged.

(11) All forms of audit trail shall be appropriately protected against unauthorised modification or deletion.

(12) Where a second level access control is implemented through the application system, password controls similar to those implemented for the computer system shall be in place.

(13) Activities of all remote users shall be logged and monitored closely.

(14) The facility to login as another user from one user's login shall be denied. However, the system should prohibit direct login as a trusted user (e.g. root in Unix, administrator in Windows NT or Windows 2000). This means that there must be a user account configured for the trusted administrator. The system requires trusted users to change their effective username to gain access to root and to re-authenticate themselves before requesting access to privileged functions.

(15) The startup and shutdown procedure of the security software must be automated.

(16) Sensitive Operating System files, which are more prone to hackers must be protected against all known attacks using proven tools and techniques. That is to say no user will be able to modify them except with the permission of System Administrator.

6.3 Password Management.—(1) Certain minimum quality standards for password shall be enforced. The quality level shall be increased progressively. The following control features shall be implemented for passwords:

(i) Minimum of eight characters without leading or trailing blanks;

(ii) Shall be different from the existing password and the two previous ones;

(iii) Shall be changed at least once every ninety days; for sensitive system, password shall be changed at least once every thirty days; and

(iv) Shall not be shared, displayed or printed.

(2) Password retries shall be limited to a maximum of three attempted logons after which the user ID shall then be revoked; for sensitive systems, the number of password retries should be limited to a maximum of two.

(3) Passwords which are easy-to-guess (e.g. user name, birth date, month, standard words etc.) should be avoided.

(4) Initial or reset passwords must be changed by the user upon first use.

(5) Passwords shall always be encrypted in storage to prevent unauthorized disclosure.

(6) All passwords used must be resistant to dictionary attacks and all known password cracking algorithms.

6.4 Privileged User's Management.—(1) System privileges shall be granted to users only on a need-to-use basis.

(2) Login privileges for highly privileged accounts should be available only from Console and terminals situated within Console room.

(3) An audit trail of activities conducted by highly privileged users shall be maintained for two years and reviewed periodically at least every week by operator who is independent of System Administrator.

(4) Privileged user shall not be allowed to log in to the computer system from remote terminal. The usage of the computer system by the privilege user shall be allowed during a certain time period.

(5) Separate user IDs shall be allowed to the user for performing privileged and normal (non-privileged) activities.

(6) The use of user IDs for emergency use shall be recorded and approved. The passwords shall be reset after use.

6.5 User's Account Management.—(1) Procedures for user account management shall be established to control access to application systems and data. The procedures shall include the following:

(i) Users shall be authorised by the computer system owner to access the computer services.

(ii A written statement of access rights shall be given to all users.

(iii) All users shall be required to sign an undertaking to acknowledge that they understand the conditions of access.

(iv) Where access to computer services is administered by service providers, ensure that the service providers do not provide access until the authorization procedures have been completed. This includes the acknowledgement of receipt of the accounts by the users.

(v) A formal record of all registered users of the computer services shall be maintained.

(vi) Access rights of users who have been transferred, or left the organisation shall be removed immediately.

(vii) A periodic check shall be carried out for redundant user accounts and access rights that are no longer required.

(viii) Ensure that redundant user accounts are not re-issued to another user.

(2) User accounts shall be suspended under the following conditions:

(i) when an individual is on extended leave or inactive use of over thirty days. In case of protected computer system, the limit of thirty days may be reduced to fifteen days by the System Administrator.

(ii) immediately upon the termination of the services of an individual.

(iii) suspended or inactive accounts shall be deleted after a two months period. In case of protected computer systems, the limit of two months may be reduced to one month.

6.6 Data and Resource Protection.—(1) All information assets shall be assigned an "owner" responsible for the integrity of that data/resource. Custodians shall be assigned and shall be jointly responsible for information assets by providing computer controls to assist owners.

(2) The operating system or security system of the computer system shall:

(i) Define user authority and enforce access control to data within the computer system;

(ii) Be capable of specifying, for each named individual, a list of named data objects (e.g. file, programme) or groups of named objects, and the type of access allowed.

(3) For networked or shared computer systems, system users shall be limited to a profile of data objects required to perform their needed tasks.

(4) Access controls for any data and/or resources shall be determined as part of the systems analysis and design process.

(5) Application Programmer shall not be allowed to access the production system.

7. Sensitive Systems Protection.—(1) Security tokens/smart cards/bio-metric technologies such as Iris recognition, finger print verification technologies etc. shall be used to complement the usage of passwords to access the computer system.

(2) For computer system processing sensitive data, access by other organisations shall be prohibited or strictly controlled.

(3) For sensitive data, encryption of data in storage shall be considered to protect its confidentiality and integrity.

8. Data Centre Operations Security

8.1 Job Scheduling.—(1) Procedures shall be established to ensure that all changes to the job schedules are appropriately approved. The authority to approve changes to job schedules shall be clearly assigned.

(2) As far as possible, automated job scheduling should be used. Manual job scheduling should require prior approval from the competent authority.

8.2 System Operations Procedure.—(1) Procedures shall be established to ensure that only authorised and correct job stream and parameter changes are made.

(2) Procedures shall be established to maintain logs of system activities. Such logs shall be reviewed by a competent independent party for indications of dubious activities. Appropriate retention periods shall be set for such logs.

(3) Procedures shall be established to ensure that people other than well-trained computer operators are prohibited from operating the computer equipment.

(4) Procedures shall be implemented to ensure the secure storage or distribution of all outputs/reports, in accordance with procedures defined by the owners for each system.

8.3 Media Management.—(1) Responsibilities for media library management and protection shall be clearly defined and assigned.

(2) All media containing sensitive data shall be stored in a locked room or cabinets, which must be fire resistant and free of toxic chemicals.

(3) Access to the media library (both on-site and off-site) shall be restricted to the authorized persons only. A list of personnel authorised to enter the library shall be maintained.

(4) The media containing sensitive and back up data must be stored at three different physical locations in the country, which can be reached in few hours.

(5) A media management system shall be in place to account for all media stored on-site and off-site.

(6) All incoming/outgoing media transfers shall be authorised by management and users.

(7) An independent physical inventory check of all media shall be conducted at least every six months.

(8) All media shall have external volume identification. Internal labels shall be fixed, where available.

(9) Procedures shall be in place to ensure that only authorised addition/removal of media from the library is allowed.

(10) Media retention periods shall be established and approved by management in accordance with legal/regulatory and user requirements.

8.4 Media Movement.—(1) Proper records of all movements of computer tapes/disks between on-site and off-site media library must be maintained.

(2) There shall be procedures to ensure the authorized and secure transfer to media to/from external parties and the off-site location. A means to authenticate the receipt shall be in place.

(3) Computer media that are being transported to off-site data backup locations should be stored in locked carrying cases that provide magnetic field protection and protection from impact while loading and unloading and during transportation.

9. Data Backup and Off-site Retention.—(1) Back-up procedures shall be documented, scheduled and monitored.

(2) Up-to-date backups of all critical items shall be maintained to ensure the continued provision of the minimum essential level of service. These items include:

(i) Data files

(ii) Utilities programmes

(iii) Databases

(iv) Operating system software

(v) Applications system software

(vi) Encryption keys

(vii) Pre-printed forms

(viii) Documentation (including a copy of the business continuity plans)

(3) One set of the original disks for all operating system and application software must be maintained to ensure that a valid, virus-free backup exists and is available for use at any time.

(4) Backups of the system, application and data shall be performed on a regular basis. Backups should also be made for application under development and data conversion efforts.

(5) Data backup is required for all systems including personal computers, servers and distributed systems and databases.

(6) Critical system data and file server software must have full backups taken weekly.

(7) The backups must be kept in an area physically separate from the server. If critical system data on the LAN represents unique versions of the information assets, then the information backups must be rotated on a periodic basis to an off-site storage location.

(8) Critical system data and file server software must have incremental backups taken daily.

(9) Systems that are completely static may not require periodic backup, but shall be backed up after changes or updates in the information.

(10) Each LAN/system should have a primary and backup operator to ensure continuity of business operations.

(11) The business recovery plan should be prepared and tested on an annual basis.

10. Audit Trails and Verification.—(1) Transactions that meet exception criteria shall be completely and accurately highlighted and reviewed by personnel independent of those that initiate the transaction.

(2) Adequate audit trails shall be captured and certain information needed to determine sensitive events and pattern analysis that would indicate possible fraudulent use of the system (e.g. repeated unsuccessful logons, access attempts over a series of days) shall be analyzed. This information includes such information as who, what, when, where, and any special information such as:

(i) Success or failure of the event

(ii) Use of authentication keys, where applicable

(3) Automated or manual procedures shall be used to monitor and promptly report all significant security events, such as accesses, which are out-of-pattern relative to time, volume, frequency, type of information asset, and redundancy. Other areas of analysis include:

(i) Significant computer system events (e.g. configuration updates, system crashes)

(ii) Security profile changes

(iii) Actions taken by computer operations, system administrators, system programmers, and/or security administrators

(4) The real time clock of the computer system shall be set accurately to ensure the accuracy of audit logs, which may be required for investigations or as evidence in legal or disciplinary cases.

(5) The real time clock of the computer or communications device shall be set to Indian Standard Time (IST). Further there shall be a procedure that checks and corrects drift in the real time clock.

(6) Computer system access records shall be kept for a minimum of two years, in either hard copy or electronic form. Records, which are of legal nature and necessary for any legal or regulation requirement or investigation of criminal behaviour, shall be retained as per laws of the land.

(7) Computer records of applications transactions and significant events must be retained for a minimum period of two years or longer depending on specific record retention requirements.

11. Measures to Handle Computer Virus.—(1) Responsibilities and duties shall be assigned to ensure that all file servers and personal computers are equipped with up-to-date virus protection and detection software.

(2) Virus detection software must be used to check storage drives both internal and external to the system on a periodic basis.

(3) All diskettes and software shall be screened and verified by virus detection software before being loaded onto the computer system. No magnetic media like tape cartridge, floppies etc. brought from outside shall be used on the data, file, PKI or computer server or personal computer on Intranet and Internet without proper screening and verification by virus detection software.

(4) A team shall be designated to deal with reported or suspected incidents of computer virus. The designated team shall ensure that latest version of anti-virus software is loaded on all data, file, PKI servers and personal computers.

(5) Procedures shall be established to limit the spread of viruses to other organization information assets. Such procedures inter alia shall include:

- (i) Communication to other business partners and users who may be at risk from an infected resource
- (ii) Eradication and recovery procedures
- (iii) Incident report must be documented and communicated per established procedures.

(6) An awareness and training programme shall be established to communicate virus protection practices, available controls, areas of high risk to virus infection and responsibilities.

12. Relocation of Hardware and Software.—Whenever computers or computer peripherals are relocated (e.g. for maintenance, installation at different sites or storage), the following guidelines shall apply:—

- (i) All removable media will be removed from the computer system and kept at secure location.

(ii) Internal drives will be overwritten, reformatted or removed as the situation may be.

(iii) If applicable, ribbons will be removed from printers.

(iv) All paper will be removed from printers.

13. Hardware and Software Maintenance.—Whenever, the hardware and software maintenance of the computer or computer network is being carried out, the following should be considered:

(1) Proper placement and installation of Information Technology equipment to reduce the effects of interference due to electromagnetic emanations.

(2) Maintenance of an inventory and configuration chart of hardware.

(3) Identification and use of security features implemented within hardware.

(4) Authorization, documentation, and control of change made to the hardware.

(5) Identification of support facilities including power and air conditioning.

(6) Provision of an uninterruptible power supply.

(7) Maintenance of equipment and services.

(8) Organisation must make proper arrangements for maintenance of computer hardware, software (both system and application) and firmware installed and used by them. It shall be the responsibility of the officer in charge of the operational site to ensure that contract for annual maintenance of hardware is always in place.

(9) Organisation must enter into maintenance agreements, if necessary, with the supplier of computer and communication hardware, software (both system and application) and firmware.

(10) Maintenance personnel will sign non-disclosure agreements.

(11) The identities of all hardware and software vendor maintenance staff should be verified before allowing them to carry out maintenance work.

(12) All maintenance personnel should be escorted within the operational site/computer system and network installation room by the authorized personnel of the organisation.

(13) After maintenance, any exposed security parameters such as passwords, user IDs, and accounts will be changed or reset to eliminate any potential security exposures.

(14) If the computer system, computer network or any of its devices is vulnerable to computer viruses as a result of performing maintenance, system managers or users shall scan the computer system and its devices and any media affected for viruses as a result of maintenance.

14. Purchase and Licensing of Hardware and Software.— (1) Hardware and software products that contain or are to be used to enforce security, and intended for use or interface into any organisation system or network, must be verified to comply with these Information Technology Security Guidelines prior to the signing of any contract, purchase or lease.

(2) Software, which is capable of bypassing or modifying the security system or operating system, integrity features, must be verified to determine that they conform to these Information Technology Security Guidelines. Where such compliance is not possible, then procedures shall be in place to ensure that the implementation and operation of that software does not compromise the security of the system.

(3) There shall be procedures to identify, select, implement and control software (system and application software) acquisition and installation to ensure compliance with the Indian Copyright Act and Information Technology Security Guidelines.

(4) It is prohibited to knowingly install on any system whether test or production, any software which is not licensed for use on the specific systems or networks.

(5) No software will be installed and used on the system when appropriate licensing agreements do not exist, except during evaluation periods for which the user has documented permission to install and test the software under evaluation.

(6) Illegally acquired or unauthorized software must not be used on any computer, computer network or data communication equipment. In the event that any illegally acquired or unauthorized software is detected by the System Administrator or Network Administrator, the same must be removed immediately.

15. System Software.—(1) All system software options and parameters shall be reviewed and approved by the management.

(2) System software shall be comprehensively tested and its security functionality validated prior to implementation.

(3) All vendor supplied default user IDs shall be deleted or password changed before allowing users to access the computer system.

(4) Versions of system software installed on the computer system and communication devices shall be regularly updated.

(5) All changes proposed in the system software must be appropriately justified and approved by an authorised party.

(6) A log of all changes to system software shall be maintained, completely documented and tested to ensure the desired results.

(7) Procedures to control changes initiated by vendors shall be in accordance with para 21 pertaining to "Change Management ".

(8) There shall be no standing "Write" access to the system libraries. All "Write" access shall be logged and reviewed by the System Administrator for dubious activities.

(9) System Programmers shall not be allowed to have access to the application system's data and programme files in the production environment.

(10) Procedures to control the use of sensitive system utilities and system programmes that could bypass intended security controls shall be in place and documented. All usage shall be logged and reviewed by the System Administrator and another person independent of System Administrator for dubious activities.

16. Documentation Security.1. Introduction.—(1) All documentation pertaining to application software and sensitive system software and changes made therein shall be updated to the current time, accurately and stored securely. An up-to-date inventory list of all documentation shall be maintained to ensure control and accountability.

(2) All documentation and subsequent changes shall be reviewed and approved by an independent authorised party prior to issue.

(3) Access to application software documentation and sensitive system software documentation shall be restricted to authorised personnel on a "need-to-use" basis only.

(4) Adequate backups of all documentation shall be maintained and a copy of all critical documentation and manuals shall be stored off-site.

(5) Documentation shall be classified according to the sensitivity of its contents/implications.

(6) Organisations shall adopt a clean desk policy for papers, diskettes and other documentation in order to reduce the risks of unauthorised access, loss of and damage to information outside normal working hours.

17. Network Communication Security.—(1) All sensitive information on the network shall be protected by using appropriate techniques. The critical network devices such as routers, switches and modems should be protected from physical damage.

(2) The network configuration and inventories shall be documented and maintained.

(3) Prior authorization of the Network Administrator shall be obtained for making any changes to the network configuration. The changes made in the network configuration shall be documented. The threat and risk assessment of the network after changes in the network configuration shall be reviewed. The network operation shall be monitored for any security irregularity. A formal procedure should be in place for identifying and resolving security problems.

(4) Physical access to communications and network sites shall be controlled and restricted to authorized individuals only in accordance with para 4.4 pertaining to "Physical Access".

(5) Communication and network systems shall be controlled and restricted to authorized individuals only in accordance with para 6.2 – System Access Control.

(6) As far as possible, transmission medium within the Certifying Authority's operational site should be secured against electro magnetic transmission. In this regard, use of Optical Fibre Cable and armoured cable may be preferred as transmission media as the case may be.

(7) Network diagnostic tools, e.g., spectrum analyzer, protocol analyzer should be used on a need basis.

18. Firewalls.—(1) Intelligent devices generally known as "Firewalls" shall be used to isolate organisation's data network with the external network. Firewall device should also be used to limit network connectivity for unauthorized use.

(2) Networks that operate at varying security levels shall be isolated from each other by appropriate firewalls. The internal network of the organization shall be physically and logically isolated from the Internet and any other external connection by a firewall.

(3) All firewalls shall be subjected to thorough test for vulnerability prior to being put to use and at least half-yearly thereafter.

(4) All web servers for access by Internet users shall be isolated from other data and host servers.

19. Connectivity.—(1) Organisation shall establish procedure for allowing connectivity of their computer network or computer system to non-organisation computer system or networks. The permission to connect other networks and computer system shall be approved by the Network Administrator and documented.

(2) All unused connections and network segments should be disconnected from active networks. The computer system/ personal computer or outside terminal accessing an organisation's host system must adhere to the general system security and access control guidelines.

(3) The suitability of new hardware/software particularly the protocol compatibility should be assessed before connecting the same to the organisation's network.

(4) As far as possible, no Internet access should be allowed to database server/ file server or server hosting sensitive data.

(5) The level of protection for communication and network resources should be commensurate with the criticality and sensitivity of the data transmitted.

20. Network Administrator.—(1) Each organization shall designate a properly trained "Network Administrator" who will be responsible for operation, monitoring security and functioning of the network.

(2) Network Administrator shall regularly undertake the review of network and also take adequate measures to provide physical, logical and procedural safeguards for its security. Appropriate follow up of any unusual activity or pattern of access on the computer network shall be investigated promptly by the Network Administrator.

(3) System must include a mechanism for alerting the Network Administrator of possible breaches in security, e.g., unauthorized access, virus infection and hacking.

(4) Secure Network Management System should be implemented to monitor functioning of the computer network. Broadcast of network traffic should be minimized.

(5) Only authorized and legal software shall be used on the network.

(6) Shared computer systems, network devices used for business applications shall comply with the requirement established in para 6 – System Integrity and Security Measures.

21. Change Management

21.1 Change Control.—(1) Procedures for tracking and managing changes in application software, system software, hardware and data in the production system shall be established. Organisational responsibilities for the change management process shall be defined and assigned.

(2) A risk and impact analysis, classification and prioritisation process shall be established.

(3) No changes to a production system shall be implemented until such changes have been formally authorised. Authorisation procedures for change control shall be defined and documented.

(4) Owners/Users shall be notified of all changes made to production system which may affect the processing of information on the said production system.

(5) Fall-back procedures in the event of a failure in the implementation of the change process shall be established and documented.

(6) Procedures to protect, control access and changes to production source code, data, execution statements and relevant system documentation shall be documented and implemented.

(7) Version changes of application software and all system software installed on the computer systems and all communication devices shall be documented. Different versions of application software and system software must be kept in safe custody.

21.2 Testing Of Changes To Production System.—(1) All changes in computer resource proposed in the production system shall be tested and the test results shall be reviewed and accepted by all concerned parties prior to implementation.

(2). All user acceptance tests in respect of changes in computer resource in production system shall be performed in a controlled environment which includes: (i) Test objectives, (ii) A documented test plan, and (iii) acceptance criteria.

21.3 Review Of Changes.—(1) Procedures shall be established for an independent review of programme changes before they are moved into a production environment to detect unauthorised or malicious codes.

(2) Procedures shall be established to schedule and review the implementation of the changes in computer resource in the production system so as to ensure proper functioning.

(3) All emergency changes/fixes in computer resource in the production system shall be reviewed and approved.

(4) Periodic management reports on the status of the changes implemented in the computer resourcde in the production system shall be submitted for management review.

22. Problem Management and Reporting.—(1) Procedures for identifying, reporting and resolving problems, such as non-functioning of Certifying Authority's system; breaches in Information Technology security; and hacking, shall be established and communicated to all personnel concerned. It shall include emergency procedures. Periodic reports shall be submitted for management review.

(2) A help desk shall be set up to assist users in the resolution of problems.

(3) A system for recording, tracking and reporting the status of reported problems shall be established to ensure that they are promptly managed and resolved with minimal impact on the user of the computing resources.

23. Emergency Preparedness.—(1) Emergency response procedures for all activities connected with computer operation shall be developed and documented. These procedures should be reviewed periodically.

(2) Emergency drills should be held periodically to ensure that the documented emergency procedures are effective.

24. Contingency Recovery Equipment and Services.—(1) Commitment shall be obtained in writing from computer equipment and supplies vendors to replace critical equipment and supplies within a specified period of time following a destruction of the computing facility.

(2) The business continuity plan shall be developed which *inter alia* include the procedures for emergency ordering of the equipment and availability of the services.

(3) The need for backup hardware and other peripherals should be evaluated in accordance to business needs.

25. Security Incident Reporting and Response.—(1) All security related incidents must be reported to a central co-ordinator, appointed by the management to co-ordinate and handle security related incidents. This central co-ordinator shall be the single point of contact at the organization.

(2) All incidents reported, actions taken, follow-up actions, and other related information shall be documented.

(3) Procedures shall be defined for dealing with all security related incidents, including malicious software, break-ins from networks, software bugs which compromised the security of the system.

26. Disaster Recovery/Management.—(1) Disaster recovery plan shall be developed, properly documented, tested and maintained to ensure that in the event of a failure of the information system or destruction of the facility, essential level of service will be provided. The disaster recovery framework should include:—

(a) emergency procedures, describing the immediate action to be taken in case of a major incident

(b) fall back procedure, describing the actions to be taken to relocate essential activities or support services to a backup site

(c) restoration procedures, describing the action to be taken to return to normal operation at the original site

(2) The documentation should include:—

(a) definition of a disaster;

(b) condition for activating the plan;

(c) stages of a crisis;

(d) who will make decisions in the crisis;

(e) role of individuals for each component of the plan;

(f) composition of the recovery team; and

(g) decision-making process for return to normal operation.

(3) Specific disaster management plan for critical applications shall be developed, documented, tested and maintained on a regular basis.

(4) Responsibilities and reporting structure shall be clearly defined which will take effect immediately on the declaration of a disaster.

(5) Each component/aspect of the plan should have a person and a backup assigned to its execution.

(6) Periodic training of personnel and users associated with computer system and network should be conducted defining their roles and responsibilities in the event of a disaster.

(7) Test plan shall be developed, documented and maintained. Periodic tests shall be carried out to test the effectiveness of the procedures in the plan. The results of the tests shall be documented for management review.

(8) Disaster recovery plan should be updated regularly to ensure its continuing effectiveness.

Schedule-III

[See rule 19(2)]

Security Guidelines for Certifying Authorities

1. Introduction.—This document prescribes security guidelines for the management and operation of Certifying Authorities (CAs) and is aimed at protecting the integrity, confidentiality and availability of their services, data and systems. These guidelines apply to Certifying Authorities that perform all the functions associated with generation, issue and management of Digital Signature Certificate such as:—

(1) Verification of registration, suspension and revocation request;

(2) Generation, issuance, suspension and revocation of Digital Signature Certificates; and

(3) Publication and archival of Digital Signature Certificates, suspension and revocation of information.

2. Security Management.—The Certifying Authority shall define Information Technology security policies for its operation on the lines defined in Schedule-II and Schedule-III. The policy shall be communicated to all personnel and widely published throughout the organisation to ensure that the personnel follow the policies.

3. Physical controls, Site Location, Construction and Physical Access.—(1) The site location, design, construction and physical security of the operational site of Certifying Authority shall be in accordance with para 4 of the Information Technology Security Guidelines given at Schedule-II.

(2) Physical access to the operational site housing computer servers, PKI server, communications and network devices shall be controlled and restricted to the authorized individuals only in accordance with para 4.4 of the Information Technology Security Guidelines given at Schedule-II.

(3) A Certifying Authority must—

(i) ensure that the operational site housing PKI servers, communications and networks is protected with fire suppression system in accordance with para 4.2 of the Information Technology Security Guidelines given at Schedule-II.

(ii) ensure that power and air-conditioning facilities are installed in accordance with para 4.1 of the Information Technology Security Guidelines given at Schedule-II.

(iii) ensure that all removable media and papers containing sensitive or plain text information are listed, documented and stored in a container properly identified.

(iv) ensure unescorted access to Certifying Authority's server is limited to those personnel identified on an access list.

(v) ensure that the exact location of Digital Signature Certification System shall not be publicly identified.

(vi) ensure that access security system is installed to control and audit access to the Digital Signature Certification System.

(vii) ensure that dual control over the inventory and access cards/keys are in place.

(viii) ensure that up-to-date list of personnel who possess the access cards/keys is maintained at the Certifying Authority's operational site. Loss of access cards/keys shall be reported immediately to the Security Administrator; who shall take appropriate actions to prevent unauthorised access.

(ix) ensure personnel not on the access list are properly escorted and supervised.

(x) ensure a site access log is maintained at the Certifying Authority's operational site and inspected periodically.

(4) Multi-tiered access mechanism must be installed at the Certifying Authority's operational site. The facility should have clearly laid out security zones within its facility with well-defined access rights to each security zone. Each security zone must be separated from the other by floor to ceiling concrete reinforced walls. Alarm and intrusion detection system must be installed at every stage with adequate power backup capable of continuing operation even in the event of loss of main power. Electrical/ Electronic circuits to external security alarm monitoring service (if used) must be supervised. No single person must have complete access to PKI Server, root keys or any computer system or network device on his/her own.

(5) Entrance to the main building where the Certifying Authority's facilities such as Data Centre, PKI Server and Network devices are housed and entrance to each security zone must be video recorded round the clock. The recording should be carefully scrutinized and maintained for at least one year.

(6) A Certifying Authority site must be manually or electronically monitored for unauthorised intrusion at all times in accordance with the Information Technology Security Guidelines given at Schedule-II.

(7) Computer System/PKI Server performing Digital Signature Certification function shall be located in a dedicated room or partition to facilitate enforcement of physical access control. The entry and exit of the said room or partition shall be automatically locked with time stamps and shall be reviewed daily by the Security Administrator.

(8) Access to infrastructure components essential to operation of Certifying Authority such as power control panels, communication infrastructure, Digital Signature Certification system, cabling, etc. shall be restricted to authorised personnel.

(9) By-pass or deactivation of normal physical security arrangements shall be authorised and documented by security personnel.

(10) Intrusion detection systems shall be used to monitor and record physical access to the Digital Signature Certification system during and after office hours.

(11) Computer System or PKI Server performing the Digital Signature Certification functions shall be dedicated to those functions and should not be used for any other purposes.

(12) System software shall be verified for integrity in accordance with para 15 of the Information Technology Security Guidelines given at Schedule-II.

4. Media Storage.—A Certifying Authority must ensure that storage media used by his system are protected from environment threats such as temperature, humidity and magnetic and are transported and managed in accordance with para 8.3 and para 8.4 of the Information Technology Security Guidelines given at Schedule-II.

5. Waste Disposal.—All media used for storage of information pertaining to all functions associated with generation, production, issue and management of Digital Signature Certificate shall be scrutinized before being destroyed or released for disposal.

6. Off-site Backup.—A Certifying Authority must ensure that facility used for off-site backup, if any, shall be within the country and shall have the same level of security as the primary Certifying Authority site.

7. Change and Configuration Management.—(1) The components of the Certifying Authority infrastructure (e.g. cryptographic algorithm and its key parameters, operating system, system software, computer system, PKI server, firewalls, physical security, system security etc.) shall be reviewed every year for new technology risks and appropriate action plan shall be developed to manage the risks identified for each component.

(2) The application software, system software and hardware, which are procured from questionable sources, shall not be installed and used for any function associated with generation and management of Digital Signature Certificate.

(3) Software updates and patches shall be reviewed for security implications before being implemented on Certifying Authority's system.

(4) Software updates and patches to rectify security vulnerability in critical systems used for Certifying Authority's operation shall be promptly reviewed and implemented.

(5) Information on the software updates and patches and their implementation on Certifying Authority's system shall be clearly and properly documented.

8. Network and Communications Security.—(1) Certifying Authority's systems shall be protected to ensure network access control to critical systems and services from other systems in accordance with para 17, para 18, para 19 and para 20 of the Information Technology Security Guidelines given at Schedule-II.

(2) Network connections from the Certifying Authority's system to external networks shall be restricted to only those connections which are essential to facilitate Certifying Authority's functional processes and services. Such network connections to the external network shall be properly secured and monitored regularly.

(3) Network connections should be initiated by the systems performing the functions of generation and management of Digital Signature Certificate to connect those systems performing the registration and repository functions but not vice versa. If this is not possible, compensating controls (e.g. use of proxy servers) shall be implemented to protect the systems performing the function of generation and management of Digital Signature Certificate from potential attacks.

(4) Systems performing the Digital Signature Certification function should be isolated to minimise their exposure to attempts to compromise the confidentiality, integrity and availability of the certification function.

(5) Communication between the Certifying Authority systems connected on a network shall be secure to ensure confidentiality and integrity of the information. For example, communications between the Certifying Authority's systems connected on a network should be encrypted and digitally signed.

(6) Intrusion detection tools should be deployed to monitor critical networks and perimeter networks and alert administrators of network intrusions and penetration attempts in a timely manner.

9. System Security Audit Procedures

9.1 Types of event recorded.—(1) The Certifying Authority shall maintain record of all events relating to the security of his system. The records should be maintained in audit log file and shall include such events as:—

(i) System start-up and shutdown;

(ii) Certifying Authority's application start-up and shutdown;

(iii) Attempts to create, remove, set passwords or change the system privileges of the PKI Master Officer, PKI Officer, or PKI Administrator;

(iv) Changes to keys of the Cerufying Authority or any of his other details;

(v) Changes to Digital Signature Certificate creation policies, e.g. validity period;

(vi) Login and logoff attempts;

(vii) Unauthorised attempts at network access to the Certifying Authority's system;

(viii) Unauthorised attempts to access system files;

(ix) Generation of own keys;

(x) Creation and revocation of Digital Signature Certificates;

(xi) Attempts to initialize remove, enable, and disable subscribers, and update and recover their keys;

(xii) Failed read-and-write operations on the Digital Signature Certificate and Certificate Revocation List (CRL) directory.

(2) Monitoring and Audit Logs

(i) A Certifying Authority should consider the use of automated security management and monitoring tools providing an integrated view of the security situation at any point in time. Records of the following application transactions shall be maintained:

(a) Registration;
(b) Certification;
(c) Publication;
(d) Suspension; and
(e) Revocation.

(ii) Records and log files shall be reviewed regularly for the following activities:

(a) Misuse;
(b) Errors;
(c) Security violations;
(d) Execution of privileged functions;
(e) Change in access control lists;
(f) Change in system configuration.

(3) All logs, whether maintained through electronic or manual means, should contain the date and time of the event, and the identity of the subscriber/subordinate/entity which caused the event.

(4) A Certifying Authority should also collect and consolidate, either electronically or manually, security information which may not be generated by his system, such as:

(i) Physical access logs;
(ii) System configuration changes and maintenance;
(iii) Personnel changes;
(iv) Discrepancy and compromise reports;
(v) Records of the destruction of media containing key material, activation data, or personal subscriber information.

(5) To facilitate decision-making, all agreements and correspondence relating to services provided by Certifying Authority should be collected and consolidated, either electronically or manually, at a single location.

9.2 Frequency of Audit Log Monitoring.—The Certifying Authority must ensure that its audit logs are reviewed by its personnel at least once every two weeks and all significant events are detailed in an audit log summary. Such reviews should involve verifying that the log has not been tampered with, and then briefly inspecting all log entries, with a more thorough investigation of any alerts or irregularities in the logs. Action taken following these reviews must be documented.

9.3 Retention Period for Audit Log.—The Certifying Authority must retain its audit logs onsite for at least twelve months and subsequently retain them in the manner described in para 10 of the Information Technology Security Guidelines as given in Schedule-II.

9.4 Protection of Audit Log.—The electronic audit log system must include mechanisms to protect the log files from unauthorized viewing, modification, and deletion.

Manual audit information must be protected from unauthorised viewing, modification and destruction.

9.5 Audit Log Backup Procedures.—Audit logs and audit summaries must be backed up or copied if in manual form.

9.6 Vulnerability Assessments.—Events in the audit process are logged, in part, to monitor system vulnerabilities. The Certifying Authority must ensure that a vulnerability assessment is performed, reviewed and revised, if necessary, following an examination of these monitored events.

10. Records Archival.—(1) Digital Signature Certificates stored and generated by the Certifying Authority must be retained for at least seven year after the date of its expiration. This requirement does not include the backup of private signature keys.

(2) Audit information as detailed in para 9, subscriber agreements, verification, identification and authentication information in respect of subscriber shall be retained for at least seven years.

(3) A second copy of all information retained or backed up must be stored at three locations within the country including the Certifying Authority site and must be protected either by physical security alone, or a combination of physical and cryptographic protection. These secondary sites must provide adequate protection from environmental threats such as temperature, humidity and magnetism. The secondary site should be reachable in few hours.

(4) All information pertaining to Certifying Authority's operation, Subscriber's application, verification, identification, authentication and Subscriber agreement shall be stored within the country. This information shall be taken out of the country only with the permission of Controller and where a properly constitutional warrant or such other legally enforceable document is produced.

(5) The Certifying Authority should verify the integrity of the backups at least once every six months.

(6) Information stored off-site must be periodically verified for data integrity.

11. Compromise and Disaster Recovery

11.1 Computing Resources, Software and/or Data are Corrupted.—The Certifying Authority must establish business continuity procedures that outline the steps to be taken in the event of the corruption or loss of computing and networking resources, nominated website, repository, software and/or data. Where a repository is not under the control of the Certifying Authority, the Certifying Authority must ensure that any agreement with the repository provides for business continuity procedures.

11.2 Secure facility after a natural or other type of disaster.—The Certifying Authority must establish a disaster recovery plan outlining the steps to be taken to re-establish a secure facility in the event of a natural or other type of disaster. Where a repository is not under the control of the Certifying Authority, the Certifying Authority must ensure that any agreement with the repository provides that a disaster recovery plan be established and documented by the repository.

11.3 Incident Management Plan.—An incident management plan shall be developed and approved by the management. The plan shall include the following areas:

(i) Certifying Authority's certification key compromise;

(ii) Hacking of systems and network;

(iii) Breach of physical security;

(iv) Infrastructure availability;

(v) Fraudulent registration and generation of Digital Signature Certificates; and

(vi) Digital Signature Certificate suspension and revocation information.

An incident response action plan shall be established to ensure the readiness of the Certifying Authority to respond to incidents. The plan should include the following areas:—

(i) Compromise control;

(ii) Notification to user community; (if applicable)

(iii) Revocation of affected Digital Signature Certificates; (if applicable)

(iv) Responsibilities of personnel handling incidents;

(v) Investigation of service disruption;

(vi) Service restoration procedure;

(vii) Monitoring and audit trail analysis; and

(viii) Media and public relations.

12. Number of Persons Required Per Task.—The Certifying Authority must ensure that no single individual may gain access to the Digital Signature Certificate server and the computer server maintaining all information associated with generation, issue and management of Digital Signature Certificate and private keys of the Certifying Authority. Minimum two individuals, preferably using a split-knowledge technique, such as twin passwords, must perform any operation associated with generation, issue and management of Digital Signature Certificate and application of private key of the Certifying Authority.

13. Identification and Authentication for Each Role.—All Certifying Authority personnel must have their identity and authorization verified before they are:—

(i) included in the access list for the Certifying Authority's site;

(ii) included in the access list for physical access to the Certifying Authority's system;

(iii) given a certificate for the performance of their Certifying Authority role;

(iv) given an account on the PKI system.

Each of these certificates and accounts (with the exception of Certifying Authority's signing certificates) must:—

(i) be directly attributable to an individual;

(ii) not be shared;

(iii) be restricted to actions authorized for that role; and

(iv) procedural controls.

Certifying Authority's operations must be secured using techniques of authentication and encryption, when accessed across-a shared network.

14. Personnel Security Controls.—The Certifying Authority must ensure that all personnel performing duties with respect to its operation must:—

(i) be appointed in writing;

(ii) be bound by contract or statute to the terms and conditions of the position they are to fill;

(iii) have received comprehensive training with respect to the duties they are to perform;

(iv) be bound by statute or contract not to disclose sensitive Certifying Authority's security related information or subscriber information;

(v) not be assigned duties that may cause a conflict of interest with their Certifying Authority's duties; and

(vi) be aware and trained in the relevant aspects of the Information Technology Security Policy and Security Guidelines framed for carrying out Certifying Authority's operation.

15. Training Requirements.—A Certifying Authority shall ensure that all personnel performing duties with respect to its operation, must receive comprehensive training in:

(i) relevant aspects of the Information Technology Security Policy and Security Guidelines framed by the Certifying Authority;

(ii) all PKI software versions in use on the Certifying Authority's system;

(iii) all PKI duties they are expected to perform; and

(iv) disaster recovery and business continuity procedures.

16. Retraining Frequency and Requirements.—The requirements of para 15 must be kept current to accommodate changes in the Certifying Authority's system. Refresher training must be conducted as and when required, and the Certifying Authority must review these requirements at least once a year.

17. Documentation Supplied to Personnel.—A Certifying Authority must make available to his personnel the Digital Signature Certificate policies it supports, its Certification Practice Statement, Information Technology Security Policy and any specific statutes, policies or contracts relevant to their position.

18. Key Management

18.1 Generation.—(1) The subscriber's key pair shall be generated by the subscriber or on a key generation system in the presence of the subscriber.

(2) The key generation process shall generate statistically random key values that are resistant to known attacks.

18.2 Distribution of Keys.—Keys shall be transferred from the key generation system to the storage device (if the keys are not stored on the key generation system) using a secure mechanism that ensures confidentiality and integrity.

18.3 Storage.—(1) Certifying Authority's keys shall be stored in tamper-resistant devices and can only be activated under split-control by parties who are not involved in the set-up and maintenance of the systems and operations of the Certifying Authority. The key of the Certifying Authority may be stored in a tamper-resistant cryptographic module or split into sub-keys stored in tamper-resistant devices under the custody of the key custodians.

(2) The Certifying Authority's key custodians shall ensure that the Certifying Authority's key component or the activation code is always under his sole custody. Change of key custodians shall be approved by the Certifying Authority's management and documented.

18.4 Usagse.—(1) A system and software integrity check shall be performed prior to Certifying Authority's key loading.

(2) Custody of and access to the Certifying Authority's keys shall be under split control. In particular, Certifying Authority's key loading shall be performed under split control.

18.5 Certifying Authority's Public key delivery to Users

The Certifying Authority's public verification key must be delivered to the prospective Digital Signature Certificate holder in an on-line transaction in accordance with PKIX-3 Certificate Management Protocol, or via an equally secure manner.

19. Private Key Protection and backup.—(1) The Certifying Authority must protect its private keys from disclosure.

(2) The Certifying Authority must back-up its private keys. Backed-up keys must be stored in encrypted form and protected at a level no lower than those followed for storing the primary version of the key.

(3) The Certifying Authority's private key backups should be stored in a secure storage facility, away from where the original key is stored.

20. Method of Destroying Private Key.—Upon termination of use of a private key, all copies of the private key in computer memory and shared disk space must be securely destroyed by over-writing. Private key destruction procedures must be described in the Certification Practice Statement or other publicly available document.

21. Usage Periods for the Public and Private Keys

21.1 Key Change.—(1) Certifying Authority and Subscriber keys shall be changed periodically.

(2) Key change shall be processed as per Key Generation guidelines.

(3) The Certifying Authority shall provide reasonable notice to the Subscriber's relying parties of any change to a new key pair used by the Certifying Authority to sign Digital Signature Certificates.

(4) The Certifying Authority shall define its key change process that ensures reliability of the process by showing how the generation of key interlocks – such as signing a hash of the new key with the old key.

All keys must have validity periods of no more than five years.

Suggested validity period:

(a) Certifying Authority's root keys and associated certificates – five years;

(b) Certifying Authority's private signing key-two years;

(c) Subscriber Digital Signature Certificate key – three years;

(d) Subscriber private key – three years.

Use of particular key lengths should be determined in accordance with departmental Threat-Risk Assessments.

21.2 Destruction.—Upon termination of use of a Certifying Authority signature private key, all components of the private key and all its backup copies shall be securely destroyed.

21.3 Key Compromise.—(1) A procedure shall be pre-established to handle cases where a compromise of the Certifying Authority's Digital Signature private key has occurred. In such case, the Certifying Authority shall immediately revoke all affected Subscriber Digital Signature Certificates.

(2) The Certifying Authority should immediately revoke the affected keys and Digital Signature Certificates in the case of Subscriber private key compromise.

(3) The Certifying Authority's public keys shall be archived permanently to facilitate audit or investigation requirements.

(4) Archives of Certifying Authority's public keys shall be protected from unauthorised modification.

22. Confidentiality of Subscriber's Information.—(1) Procedures and security controls to protect the privacy and confidentiality of the subscribers' data under the Certifying Authority's custody shall be implemented. Confidential information provided by the subscriber must not be disclosed to a third party without the subscribers' consent, unless the information is required to be disclosed under the law or a court order.

(2) Data on the usage of the Digital Signature Certificates by the subscribers and other transactional data relating to the subscribers' activities generated by the Certifying Authority in the course of its operation shall be protected to ensure the subscribers' privacy.

(3) A secure communication channel between the Certifying Authority and its subscribers shall be established to ensure the authenticity, integrity and confidentiality of the exchanges (e.g. transmission of Digital Signature Certificate, password, private key) during the Digital Signature Certificate issuance process.

Note

Index